The Stewart English Program

Book 1
Principles Plus ...

Donald S. Stewart

About the author: Donald S. Stewart taught English at Belmont Hill School, an independent school for boys in Belmont, Massachusetts. In 1990 he founded Write for College, an intensive summer writing course that he directed for 25 years, preparing high school students from the Boston area for the writing challenges of college and beyond. In 2015 he took the course online at http://writingwhatever.com.

ISBN: 978-1-63263-855-7

Published by BookLocker.com, Inc., St. Petersburg, Florida.

Printed on acid-free paper.

BookLocker.com, Inc.
2018

Second edition

Cover designed by Shar www.fiverr.com/landofawes

CONTENTS

INTRODUCTION

I have always been intrigued by the question put to me years ago by a colleague, a biology teacher. "What animals," he asked, "were the last to learn about the ocean?" Birds, he then explained, knew about the ocean because they had seen it from the air. The creatures dwelling on land knew about it because they had walked along the shore. But because they were immersed in it, living in it and breathing it, the animals that learned last about the sea that surrounded them, that touched them every moment of their lives, were the fish.

We are like those fish, and the sea we swim in is our English language. We are born into it, frolic in it, occasionally get lost in it, and grow in it. And finally there comes the time when we begin to learn about it. We learn the names of the parts, how those parts work together, and how to make them work for us. That is why this series is called *Principles Plus*, *Grammar Plus*, and *Writing Plus*.

I wish to express my indebtedness to the late Francis Christensen and his wife, Bonniejean, for the inspiration for these textbooks. *Writing Plus*, the third in the series, is my revision of their masterpiece, *The Christensen Rhetoric Program*, which proved beyond a doubt that writing can be taught actively, not just reactively. Their method, of observation, discovery, and assimilation, is the most natural of learning styles for the young people who stand at the threshold of opportunity and responsibility as the writers of the future.

May I also thank the many students I taught at Belmont Hill School over the years, for their encouragement, their enthusiasm in collecting the sample sentences from their favorite books, and their willingness to be the most honest of critics as I refined my presentation. The sparkle in their eyes has been my greatest reward.

Donald S. Stewart

1. VERBS

> ## A verb is a word or group of words used to express an action or a state of being.

If you want to say something intelligent to a friend using the fewest number of words, you can do it with just one word.

Look.   *Stay.*   *Hurry!*   *Go!*   *Jump!*

These are all one-word sentences, and that one word is a **verb**. A sentence expresses a complete thought, and if you walk up to your friend and say, "Watch," your friend will probably do just that. Your friend would look at you with a rather puzzled expression if you said, "Dictionary" or "Nevertheless" or "Purple." That's because those single words are not complete thoughts.

Usually, however, a sentence contains more than one word. We hear two-word sentences all the time:

I tried.   *Sally left?*   *Cows moo.*   *Ice melts.*   *Justice prevailed.*

From here you may continue to add words, making your sentences more elaborate, interesting, and exact. But the heart of the sentence remains the verb. Simply put, without the verb, there would be no sentence.

Before we go any further, let's take a closer look at the definition of a verb at the top of this page. It says that a verb *expresses action* or *state of being*. **Action verbs** tell about an activity, something that we *do* or that *happens* around us.

I *slept* until noon.   The fire alarm *rang*.   We *considered* our options.

By *state of being* we mean, not that the subject is *doing* something, but simply that the subject is *being* something. What follows the verb will either restate the subject or describe the subject—in other words, tell what the subject is *being*. These verbs are often called **linking verbs**, because they link the subject with that later information. The most common linking verbs are *be, look, sound, taste, feel, smell, appear, remain, grow, prove, turn, seem,* and *become*.

That policeman is my father.	(the policeman is *being* my father)
Your finger looks swollen.	(your finger, maybe, is *being* swollen)
We became dizzy on the Tilt-a-Whirl.	(You were *being* dizzy)

PRINCIPAL PARTS OF THE VERB

When you look up a verb in the dictionary, in addition to the pronunciation guide and the definition, you will see the **principal parts of the verb**. By knowing the principal parts, you can use a verb in any way that you wish. All verbs have four principal parts: **infinitive**, **past**, **past participle**, and **present participle**.

1. **Infinitive**: The infinitive is the form we use to find a verb in the dictionary. From it we create the present tense, adding *-s* or *-es* when the subject is *he*, *she*, or *it*.

I *ride*	we *ride*
you *ride*	you *ride*
he, she, it *rides*	they *ride*

There is one very important exception to this pattern, the verb *be*.

I *am*	we *are*
you *are*	you *are*
he, she, it *is*	they *are*

The infinitive is also the verb form we use to give commands. These are called **imperative** sentences, and the subject is the understood pronoun *you,* either singular or plural.

Take me out to the ball game.
Please *help* me with this equipment.
Go, team!

2. **Past:** As we consider the other verb forms, we discover that some verbs are predictable and others are not. For a **regular verb,** the past form is simply the infinitive with an *-ed* ending. Sometimes there is a spelling change because of the ending.

talk/talked	*paint/painted*	*wander/wandered*
trip/tripped	*trade/traded*	*try/tried*

With an **irregular verb,** however, the past tense does not follow a predictable pattern and therefore must be learned.

ride/rode	*eat/ate*	*go/went*

One more thing: the verb *be* has two past forms, *was* and *were*.

3. **Past participle:** For a regular verb, the past participle looks exactly the same as the past form. The past participle is the form that you would use in expressions like *I have_____* .

talk/ have talked	*paint/ have painted*	*wander/ have wandered*
trip/ have tripped	*trade/ have traded*	*try/ have tried*

The past participle of an irregular verb, however, is almost always unpredictable.

eat/ have eaten	*go/ have gone*	*catch/ have caught*

4. **Present participle:** No matter whether the verb is regular or irregular, the present participle form is made the same way. Simply take the infinitive and add *-ing*. This is the form that you would use in expressions such as *I am _____* . Once again the spelling may vary because of the ending.

deliver/delivering	*write/writing*	*hit/hitting*

VERBS

Name: _____

EXERCISE A: principal parts

Accuracy _____

Directions: Look up the following irregular verbs in a dictionary and determine their principal parts. Fill in the blanks with the correct forms. If there are alternative forms of any principal part, write them both and notice if one is preferred. You will be graded only on accuracy.

Infinitive	Past	Past participle (used with *has / have / had*)	Present participle (used with *am / is / are was / were / will be*)
begin			
blow			
break			
choose			
drink			
freeze			
know			
lead			
lose			
ring			
rise			
run			
see			
set			
speak			
stink			
swim			
think			
throw			
write			

EXERCISE B: writing with irregular verbs   **Accuracy** _____ **Creativity** _____

Directions: In the spaces below, write sentences using the given irregular verbs or verb phrases as the main verbs. Notice that you will be graded on both accuracy and creativity.

1. _____
                                (had swum)
    _____

2. _____
                              (is beginning)
    _____

3. _____
                                (has drunk)
    _____

4. _____
                              (are choosing)
    _____

5. _____
                                (have led)
    _____

6. _____
                              (had broken)
    _____

7. _____
                                 (threw)
    _____

8. _____
                               (has risen)
    _____

9. _____
                                 (froze)
    _____

10. _____
                             (will be ringing)
    _____

TENSES OF THE VERB

When we talk about the **tense** of a verb, we are talking about when that verb happened.

There are six main verb tenses: **past**, **present**, **future**, **past perfect**, **present perfect**, and **future perfect**.

The perfect tenses show a verb that is finished or completed (perfected) before another verb began. (Example: They *had eaten* before I *arrived*.) These tenses use the past participle form of the verb.

Each of the six main tenses also has an additional form, the **progressive**, which shows that the verb is still in progress and not yet completed. (Example: They *were eating* when I *arrived*.) The progressive uses the present participle *(-ing)* form of the verb.

Here are two verbs, the regular verb *walk* and the irregular verb *ride*, in all twelve tenses, using *they* as the subject.

Past:	They walked.	They rode.
Past progressive:	They were walking.	They were riding.
Present:	They walk.	They ride.
Present progressive:	They are walking.	They are riding.
Future:	They will walk.	They will ride.
Future progressive:	They will be walking.	They will be riding.
Past perfect:	They had walked.	They had ridden.
Past perfect progressive:	They had been walking.	They had been riding.
Present perfect:	They have walked.	They have ridden.
Present perfect progressive:	They have been walking.	They have been riding.
Future perfect:	They will have walked.	They will have ridden.
Future perfect progressive:	They will have been walking.	They will have been riding.

HELPING VERBS

In the examples above, we added helping verbs to the main verb to make the different tenses. Besides the various forms of *be* and *have*, there are some other helping verbs.

1. **Do, does, did:** This helper is used to ask a question, to form the negative, or to add emphasis to the main verb. It accompanies the infinitive form of the verb.

   Do you *know* where I left my science book?

   Does everyone going on the field trip to the museum *have* a ticket?

   Did either of the flashlights *come* with batteries?

   Most of the teachers *did* not *agree* with the principal.

   Yes, this model *does feature* a back-up camera.

   I *do want* to meet her as soon as she arrives.

2. **Modals:** A modal is a helping verb that shows degrees of possibility or obligation for the verb to happen.

can	shall	will
could	*should*	*would*
might	*must*	*may*

None of us *can see* him while he is in intensive care.

None of us *will see* him while he is in intensive care.

Could I *meet* you in the lobby?

Should I *meet* you in the lobby?

We all *might go* to the lake.

We all *must go* to the lake.

Unlike the other helping verbs, modals do not have any other forms, and they never stand alone. There are no such words as *to could, coulding, coulded,* or *coulds.*

Modals often combine with the regular helpers, forms of *be* and *have.*

might be going   *might have gone*   *might have been going*

3. **The *to* helpers:** There are several helpers that include the word *to.* They are followed by the infinitive form of the verb. But remember that the *to* is part of the helper, not part of the main verb.

has to	have to	had to
ought to	*used to*	*going to*

We *have to sign up* by Wednesday for the spectator bus.

You *ought to try* this new mechanical pencil.

Rachel *used to drive* to work every day, but now she is *going to start* riding the subway.

HELPING VERB ISSUES

There are several important points to notice about helping verbs. First, when you are trying to determine the verb of a sentence, be sure to include all the helping verbs along with the main verb. This is called the **verb phrase.** In the examples above, the verb phrase is shown in *italics.* Be especially alert when the words of the verb phrase do not immediately follow one another, such as in questions or when there are other sentence elements separating them.

Remember that *be, have,* and *do* may be either main verbs or helping verbs. Compare the following sentences:

***was* as helping verb**	Everyone *was standing.*
***was* as main verb**	Everyone *was* happy.

***had* as helping verb**	I *had eaten* the pancakes.
***had* as main verb**	I *had* pancakes.

***does* as helping verb**	This bank *does* not *charge* a service fee.
***does* as main verb**	This bank *does* a lot for this community.

VERBS

Name: _____

EXERCISE C: writing verb tenses

Accuracy _____ **Creativity** _____

Directions: In this exercise we have provided irregular verbs in a specific tense. You are to write a sentence using that verb as the main verb. Then, in the space at the end of the sentence, tell what tense that verb is, using the appropriate letter from the list below. Notice that you will be graded on both accuracy and creativity.

A. Past	**B. Present**	**C. Future**
D. Past Perfect	**E. Present Perfect**	**F. Future Perfect**
G. Past Progressive	**H. Present Progressive**	**I. Future Progressive**
J. Past Perfect Progressive	**K. Present Perfect Progressive**	**L. Future Perfect Progressive**

1.   (loses)_____

   _____ _____
                                                                (tense)

2.   (have set) _____

   _____ _____
                                                                (tense)

3.   (will write) _____

   _____ _____
                                                                (tense)

4.   (was running)_____

   _____ _____
                                                                (tense)

5.   (stinks)_____

   _____ _____
                                                                (tense)

6.   (will have been hiking)_____

   _____ _____
                                                                (tense)

7.   (will think)_____

   _____ _____
                                                                (tense)

8.   (has seen)_____

   _____ _____
                                                                (tense)

9. (blew) _____

_____ _____
(tense)

10. (will have spoken) _____

_____ _____
(tense)

VERBS

Name: _____

EXERCISE D: verb phrases

Accuracy _____ **Creativity** _____

Directions: In the sentences below, fill in each blank with a verb phrase in the tense or form indicated that will logically complete the meaning of the sentence.

1. My brother's band _____ at the town hall this Saturday night.
   (future)

2. The sprinkler _____ all day.
   (present perfect progressive)

3. I _____ not yet _____ a good summer job.
   (present   perfect)

4. His father's company _____ an amazing new app.
   (past perfect)

5. You _____ perfectly happy with your *C-* in Social Studies.
   (present)

6. Several of the runners _____ before the race.
   (past progressive)

7. Someone in the house next door _____ .
   (present progressive)

8. Your aunt from Houston _____ tomorrow morning.
   (future progressive)

9. Any student wanting to go on the ski trip _____ by Thursday.
   (modal + infinitive)

10. _____ you ever _____ in a cave before?
    (present   perfect)

11. This new magazine _____ not _____ much news.
    (does *or* did)   *(infinitive)*

12. You _____ with me.
    (future perfect progressive)

13. The soldiers _____ throughout the night.
    (past perfect)

14. Please _____ .
    (infinitive)

15. _____ they _____ ?
    (past   perfect progressive)

16. _____ he _____ you?
    (modal)   (infinitive)

17. Without that information, we never _____ it.
    (modal + present perfect)

18. I realize now that I _____ instead.
    (modal + present perfect progressive)

19. _____ !
    (infinitive)

20. Most of the students still _____ before they can go.
    (modal + infinitive)

2. NOUNS AND PREPOSITIONS

A noun is a word used to identify a person, place, thing, or idea.

There are two distinct categories of nouns, the **common noun** and the **proper noun**. A **common noun** is a word used to identify a person, place, thing, or idea, in general. It is not capitalized.

People:	sister	uncle	plumber	actor	nurse
Places:	village	airport	mountain	theater	cave
Things:	shoes	sandwich	painting	book	game
Ideas:	love	kindness	fear	courage	honor

A **proper noun** is a word used to identify a specific person, place, thing, or idea. It is capitalized. If it is more than one word, such as the name of a story, the first word will be capitalized, and so will the other important words.

NOUNS AND PREPOSITIONS

Name: _____

EXERCISE A: common and proper nouns

Accuracy _____ Creativity _____

Directions: Here is a list of common nouns. Fill in the blank next to each one with a proper noun that is a specific example of it. Remember that proper nouns are capitalized. Compare your answers with those from others in your class.

	Common Noun	**Proper Noun**
1	friend	
2	teacher	
3	school	
4	street	
5	magazine	
6	queen	
7	novel	
8	automobile	

	Common Noun	Proper Noun
9	candy	
10	company	
11	month	
12	athlete	
13	TV show	
14	newspaper	
15	poem	
16	capital of a country	
17	actor	
18	team	
19	language	
20	planet	
21	short story	
22	ship	
23	scientist	
24	house of worship	
25	country	
26	rock band	
27	computer game	
28	holiday	
29	play	
30	state	
31	river	
32	college	
33	cartoon character	

THE SUBJECT AND THE PREDICATE

1. **Subject:** There are two basic parts to every sentence, the subject and the predicate. The **subject** of a sentence will often be a noun. It is the person, place, thing, or idea about which the sentence is making a statement or asking a question. The simple subject will be the noun by itself. The **complete subject** is the simple subject, plus any other words associated with it.

    When you need to determine the simple subject of a sentence, ask yourself a question: "Who or what is being spoken about?" Look at the following examples and see how asking that question leads to identifying correctly the simple subject of the sentence. We have written the simple subject in *italics* and put [brackets] around the complete subject.

    > [Our next-door *neighbors*] have invited us to a cookout.
    > In the bowl on the dining room table were [two ripe *bananas*].
    > [Most *members* of the choir] also play an instrument.

2. **Predicate:** The predicate of a sentence is what is being said about the subject. The **simple predicate** is the verb or verb phrase of the sentence, and the complete predicate is everything that is being said about the complete subject. Here are the example sentences again. This time, the simple predicate is in *italics* and the complete predicate is in [brackets]. Compare the two.

    > Our next-door neighbors [*have invited* us to a cookout].
    > [In the bowl on the dining room table *were*] two ripe bananas.
    > Most members of the choir [also *play* an instrument].

Name: _____

EXERCISE B: subjects and predicates   Accuracy _____ Creativity _____

Directions: For 1–10, we have supplied the complete subject of a sentence, but no predicate. For 11–20, we have supplied the complete predicate, but no subject. You are to supply a complete subject or predicate that logically and creatively completes the sentence. Be able to identify the simple subject and the simple predicate in each sentence.

1. The three kittens in the basket _____

    _____ .

2. My homework assignment for English _____

    _____ .

3. Most people who have traveled around the country _____

    _____ .

4. The present hidden on the top shelf of my closet _____

    _____ .

5. _____ your uncle _____ ?

6.   The girl sitting in the front row _____

   _____ .

7.   Doctors _____

   _____ .

8.   My favorite animals in the zoo _____

   _____ .

9.   These shoes, which I just bought last Saturday, _____

   _____ .

10. Sara's winning goal in yesterday's semifinals _____

   _____ .

11. _____

   _____ isn't worth very much.

12. _____

   _____ should go to the office after this class.

13. _____

   _____ discovered a skeleton in the cave.

14. _____

   _____ is on page seventeen.

15. _____ left.

16. _____

   _____ has taken all the good ones.

17. _____

   _____ forgot to close the door.

18. _____

   _____looks wonderful.

19. _____

   _____ serves the best frozen yogurt.

20. _____

   _____ was my all-time favorite.

OTHER NOUNS IN THE SENTENCE

1. **Direct object:** Very often a sentence will tell us that a noun is performing an action, and that some other noun is receiving that action. The noun that is doing the action is the subject, and the noun receiving the action is the **direct object**.

    Again, asking a question can help us locate the direct object in a sentence. Ask yourself this: "Who or what is receiving the action that the subject is doing?" Or a more memorable question: "Who or what is getting verbed?" Consider how asking that question helps to locate the direct objects in these examples.

Jeremy carefully hung his clean *clothes* on coat hangers.	(hung what?)
Did the trash men take away the old *tires?*	(did take away what?)
I have written two more *poems* for the school literary magazine.	(have written what?)
She sells *seashells* by the seashore.	(sells what?)

2. **Indirect object:** So far we have talked about two uses of the noun, as a subject performing an action, and as a direct object receiving that action. In addition, some sentences contain a noun that tells *to whom* or *for whom* that action was done. This noun is called the **indirect object**, and it always precedes the direct object. In fact, it is impossible to have an indirect object without a direct object.

    The question we use to locate the indirect object builds on what we already know about the rest of the sentence: "The subject performed an action, and the direct object received that action. *To whom* or *for whom* was that action performed?" Here are some examples of sentences that contain indirect objects. First, try to find the subjects and the direct objects. Then it will be easy to identify the indirect objects.

We gave the *singer* a standing ovation.
Did you tell your *girlfriend* the combination to your lock?
I bought my *brother* a skateboard for his birthday.
The coach showed the *team* a new formation.

3. **Predicate noun:** Up until now, we have been talking about sentences that have action, and about the doers and receivers of that action. However, as you learned in Chapter 1, "Verbs," sometimes the subject of a sentence is not *doing* something, but is *being* something. When that something is a noun in the predicate, it is called the **predicate noun**. The predicate noun restates in a different way the person, place, thing, or idea that is the subject.

    Predicate nouns are quite common, but they follow only linking verbs. They most often are used with forms of *be: am, is, are, was, were, will be, has been, is being, could have been,* etc.

    They may also be used with the linking verbs *seem, become, remain, stay,* and *prove.*
Here are some examples.

My favorite teacher in the whole school is *Mrs. Patel.*
"I could have been a *contender,*" says Marlon Brando in *On the Waterfront.*
His idea to paint his car himself proved a *disaster.*
Even after she moved to Minnesota, Rene remained my best *friend.*

NOUNS AND PREPOSITIONS

Name: _____

EXERCISE C: direct objects, indirect objects, and predicate nouns

Accuracy _____ **Creativity** _____

Directions: In the following sentences, fill in the blanks using nouns as indicated. You may also write whatever additional words you feel are appropriate to describe the nouns you have selected.

1. May I have _____
    (direct object)

    _____ .

2. Give _____ _____
    (indirect object)   *(direct object)*

    _____ .

3. The first contestant will be _____
    (predicate noun)

    _____ .

4. After college my aunt became _____
    (predicate noun)

    _____ .

5. The police found _____
    (direct object)

    _____ .

6. The coach bought _____ _____
    (indirect object)   *(direct object)*

    _____ .

7. Our car needs _____
    (direct object)

    _____ .

8. You shouldn't show _____ _____
    (indirect object)   *(direct object)*

    _____ .

9. Even after retirement he remained a(n) _____
    (predicate noun)

    _____ .

10. Please tell _____ _____
    (indirect object)   *(direct object)*

    _____ .

4. **Noun of direct address:** When you speak to people, you often call them by their name, their title, their nickname, or their relationship to you. Those are all nouns, and because you are addressing these people directly, they are called **nouns of direct address**. An important punctuation rule is that such a noun is set off from the rest of the sentence by a comma. If the noun of direct address is someplace other than at the beginning or end of a sentence, there is a comma on each side of it.

"*Miss Bolton*, will you be available for extra help after lunch today?"

"Yes, *sir*, I heard the question."

"Of course, *Mother*, we won't stay out too late."

"We're ready to land, *Captain*."

5. **Appositive:** Many times in a sentence we will want to refer to a noun in more than one way, perhaps first as a common noun and then as a proper noun, or first as a simple noun and then as a phrase. Repeating an idea using different words is an efficient and stylish way to say exactly what you want. Such a repeated noun is called an **appositive**. In the following sentences, the appositives are in *italics*. What noun is being repeated in each sentence?

Have you seen my new puppy, *Samson*?

The capital of Massachusetts, *Boston*, is sometimes called the "Athens of America."

Have you met my friend *Jennifer*?

In Shakespeare's play *The Merchant of Venice* we hear Portia's famous "Mercy" speech.

Notice that the first two examples used commas, and the second two did not. If the appositive is not essential, but just additional information, use commas. (I have only one new puppy; Massachusetts has only one capital.) If the appositive is essential to our understanding of the sentence, do not set off the appositive with commas. (I have more than one friend; Shakespeare wrote several plays.)

A preposition is a word that shows a relationship between a noun or pronoun and another word in the sentence.

6. **Object of the preposition:** In order to present the final function of the noun, we need to introduce a third part of speech, the **preposition**. Together, the preposition and the noun (or pronoun—see Chapter 6) combine to form one of the most common and useful grammatical units, the **prepositional phrase**. The noun or pronoun that follows the preposition is called the **object of the preposition**.

It is helpful to remember that the word *preposition* is based on the word *position*. A prepositional phrase is often used to show *position in space* or *position in time*.

Below is a list of prepositions that show position in space. Imagine that a butterfly has come into your home. It flew *through the window*. Where else could it fly?

about	above	across	against	along	among	around	at
behind	below	beneath	beside	between	beyond	by	down
from	in	into	near	off	on	outside	over
past	round	through	to	toward	under	underneath	up
upon	within	without					

Here are the prepositions that show position in time. Think about this phrase: *the championship game.* Now put each of the following prepositions before it and notice how the meaning changes.

after   before   during   since   till   until

There are also a few prepositions that show a relationship that is more abstract. With these, imagine the word *love* as the object of the preposition.

as	*besides*	*but*	*concerning*	*except*	*for*	*like*
of	*regarding*	*with*	*upon*	*within*	*without*	

Sometimes two or more words combine to form what is considered a single preposition.

because of	*on account of*	*by means of*	*in spite of*	*apart from*
in place of	*instead of*	*according to*	*out of*	

In the following examples, we have identified the nouns in the sentence that are the objects of prepositions. Can you identify which preposition goes with each object?

The drone in the *catalog* does not come with *batteries.*
In spite of her *warnings*, he dived into the *quarry pond.*
The audience at the *concert* was impressed by the *drum solo.*
According to the *polls*, the candidates are tied in the *senate race.*

MULTIPLE NOUNS

In all of the examples we have seen so far, we have seen only one noun as the subject, direct object, and so forth. Many times, however, there will be more than one noun performing a particular function. In such cases, we have what is called a **compound** subject, direct object, and so forth. Consider these examples:

compound subject	*Karen* and her *father* were planning the refreshments.
compound direct object	They needed *drinks, chips,* and *dip* to go with the sandwiches.
compound indirect object	They gave *Sal* and his *brother* some money to buy those things.
compound predicate noun	The best drinks were the *juices* and the *cider.*
compound noun of direct address	"Friends, *Romans, countrymen,* lend me your ears," yells Marc Antony after the murder of Julius Caesar.
compound appositive	My dog is a mix of two breeds, a *husky* and a *golden retriever.*
compound object of a preposition	We all were delighted with the *music* and the *dancing.*

NOUNS AND PREPOSITIONS

Name: _____

EXERCISE D: writing with nouns

Accuracy _____ **Creativity** _____

Directions: Here, we have provided some nouns and indicated where they go in the sentence. You are to write a sentence that uses those words in the correct places. After you have satisfied the requirements of the sentence, you may add additional ideas of your own. **Notice that some sentences are questions, as indicated by the question mark.** You will be graded on both accuracy and creativity.

Example:
student	*blackboard*	*class*
(subject)	(direct object)	(object of prep.)

Any student who is late to Miss Shaw's class must wash her blackboard.

1.
professor	class	armor	Middle Ages
(subject)	(indirect object)	(direct object)	(object of prep.)

_____

_____

2.
friend	programmer	company
(subject)	(predicate noun)	(object of prep.)

_____

_____

3.
aunt	Sylvia	advice	sister	driving
(subject)	(indirect object)	(direct object)	(appositive)	(object of prep.)

_____

_____

4.
director	Mrs. Worthington	actors	costumes, props
(subject)	(noun of direct address)	(indirect object)	(direct object)

_____

_____

5.
| dogs, cats | owners | nightmares | neighbors |
| *(compound subjects)* | *(indirect object)* | *(direct object)* | *(object of prep.)* |

_____

_____

_____ **?**

6.
| Denise, Jim | Joyce | Steven |
| *(compound subjects)* | *(direct object)* | *(object of prep.)* |

_____

_____

_____ **?**

7.
| subject | honesty | government |
| *(subject)* | *(predicate noun)* | *(object of prep.)* |

_____

_____

_____

8.
| sergeant | recruits | instructions | plane |
| *(subject)* | *(indirect object)* | *(direct object)* | *(object of prep.)* |

_____

_____

_____

9.
| spider | scouts | tent | camping trip |
| *(subject)* | *(direct object)* | *(object of prep.)* | *(object of prep.)* |

_____

_____

_____

10.
| movie | mystery | London, Paris | cities |
| *(subject)* | *(predicate noun)* | *(compound object of prep.)* | *(appositive)* |

_____

_____

_____

NOUNS AND PREPOSITIONS

Name: _____

EXERCISE E: identifying the functions of nouns

Accuracy _____ **Creativity** _____

Directions: For each of the sentences below, write in the blanks the nouns that are performing each of the indicated functions. If there is any kind of compound, separate the nouns with a comma; if there is more than one prepositional phrase, write the objects of the different prepositions with a slanted line between them. Notice that you will be graded only on accuracy.

Examples: On Tuesday the painter gave my father the estimate for the job.

__painter__	__father__	__estimate__	_____
(subject)	*(indirect object)*	*(direct object)*	*(predicate noun)*

Tuesday / job	_____	_____
(object of prep.)	*(noun of direct address)*	*(appositive)*

My history teacher, Dr. Manuelian, could have become a lawyer in New York.

__teacher__	_____	_____	__lawyer__
(subject)	*(indirect object)*	*(direct object)*	*(predicate noun)*

New York	_____	Dr. Manuelian
(object of prep.)	*(noun of direct address)*	*(appositive)*

1. The astronauts circled the earth for seven days before their return.

_____	_____	_____	_____
(subject)	*(indirect object)*	*(direct object)*	*(predicate noun)*

_____	_____	_____
(object of prep.)	*(noun of direct address)*	*(appositive)*

2. By the end of the game, both teams, the Patriots and the Jaguars, were covered with mud.

_____	_____	_____	_____
(subject)	*(indirect object)*	*(direct object)*	*(predicate noun)*

_____	_____	_____
(object of prep.)	*(noun of direct address)*	*(appositive)*

3. "Officer, did Mrs. Corbett, my neighbor, ever identify the person who peered into her window?"

_____	_____	_____	_____
(subject)	*(indirect object)*	*(direct object)*	*(predicate noun)*

_____	_____	_____
(object of prep.)	*(noun of direct address)*	*(appositive)*

4. Both Dave and Karl bought their sisters the same umbrellas for Christmas.

          _____   _____   _____   _____

             (subject)   *(indirect object)*   *(direct object)*   *(predicate noun)*

          _____   _____   _____

       (object of prep.)   *(noun of direct address)*   *(appositive)*

5. Samantha has always been a very good student in Spanish.

             (subject)   *(indirect object)*   *(direct object)*   *(predicate noun)*

       (object of prep.)   *(noun of direct address)*   *(appositive)*

6. In 1992 the nation elected Bill Clinton for president instead of the incumbent, George H.W. Bush.

             (subject)   *(indirect object)*   *(direct object)*   *(predicate noun)*

       (object of prep.)   *(noun of direct address)*   *(appositive)*

7. Grandmother always knits her grandchildren beautiful sweaters for their birthdays.

             (subject)   *(indirect object)*   *(direct object)*   *(predicate noun)*

       (object of prep.)   *(noun of direct address)*   *(appositive)*

8. The nurse put iodine and a bandage on my little finger.

             (subject)   *(indirect object)*   *(direct object)*   *(predicate noun)*

       (object of prep.)   *(noun of direct address)*   *(appositive)*

9. According to our records, your company owes the state $3000 in back taxes.

             (subject)   *(indirect object)*   *(direct object)*   *(predicate noun)*

       (object of prep.)   *(noun of direct address)*   *(appositive)*

10. Before swimming in the pool, all guests must take a shower.

_____   _____   _____   _____
(subject)   *(indirect object)*   *(direct object)*   *(predicate noun)*

_____   _____   _____
(object of prep.)   *(noun of direct address)*   *(appositive)*

11. Dad left the children some dinner in the refrigerator, lasagna and cheesecake.

_____   _____   _____   _____
(subject)   *(indirect object)*   *(direct object)*   *(predicate noun)*

_____   _____   _____
(object of prep.)   *(noun of direct address)*   *(appositive)*

12. Without warning, the science teacher closed her book, grabbed her coat, and left the room.

_____   _____   _____   _____
(subject)   *(indirect object)*   *(direct object)*   *(predicate noun)*

_____   _____   _____
(object of prep.)   *(noun of direct address)*   *(appositive)*

13. Only two people have volunteered for working on the rummage sale, Ms. Dale and Mr. Evans.

_____   _____   _____   _____
(subject)   *(indirect object)*   *(direct object)*   *(predicate noun)*

_____   _____   _____
(object of prep.)   *(noun of direct address)*   *(appositive)*

14. After her game-winning basket, the team gave Mavis a nickname, "Hoops."

_____   _____   _____   _____
(subject)   *(indirect object)*   *(direct object)*   *(predicate noun)*

_____   _____   _____
(object of prep.)   *(noun of direct address)*   *(appositive)*

15. Suddenly, through the door walked two masked men with guns.

_____   _____   _____   _____
(subject)   *(indirect object)*   *(direct object)*   *(predicate noun)*

_____   _____   _____
(object of prep.)   *(noun of direct address)*   *(appositive)*

16. At yesterday's game the ushers gave the first one thousand fans miniature baseball bats.

_____	_____	_____	_____
(subject)	*(indirect object)*	*(direct object)*	*(predicate noun)*

_____	_____	_____
(object of prep.)	*(noun of direct address)*	*(appositive)*

17. "Mom, the area code listed in your smart phone is not the right number."

_____	_____	_____	_____
(subject)	*(indirect object)*	*(direct object)*	*(predicate noun)*

_____	_____	_____
(object of prep.)	*(noun of direct address)*	*(appositive)*

18. My father's boss has been his close friend since their days together in college.

_____	_____	_____	_____
(subject)	*(indirect object)*	*(direct object)*	*(predicate noun)*

_____	_____	_____
(object of prep.)	*(noun of direct address)*	*(appositive)*

19. "Sorry, Mr. Stebbins, but without water or sunlight, your plants have simply died."

_____	_____	_____	_____
(subject)	*(indirect object)*	*(direct object)*	*(predicate noun)*

_____	_____	_____
(object of prep.)	*(noun of direct address)*	*(appositive)*

20. "Is your name Angelina, young lady?"

_____	_____	_____	_____
(subject)	*(indirect object)*	*(direct object)*	*(predicate noun)*

_____	_____	_____
(object of prep.)	*(noun of direct address)*	*(appositive)*

3. ADJECTIVES

An adjective is a word or group of words used to modify a noun or pronoun.

When we say that an adjective is used to *modify* a noun or a pronoun, we mean that it helps to clarify, limit, define, or otherwise describe that noun or pronoun. An adjective will usually answer one of these questions: *Which one? What kind? How many?* or *How much?*

1. **Limiting adjectives:** A limiting adjective is any of a wide variety of words that identify and limit a noun or pronoun, but which do not really describe it. The limiting adjectives fall into several categories.

Articles:	*a, an, the*
Demonstratives:	*this, that, these, those, a certain*
Possessives:	*my, your, his, her, its, our, their, whose, NOUN+'s*
Ordinals:	*first, second, third...next, last*
Quantifiers:	*one, two, three, each, every, both, only, few, little, some, several, many, most, all, any, another, no*
Comparatives and superlatives:	*more, most, less, least, fewer, fewest*

Be careful when identifying these words as adjectives. Be sure that they are, in fact, modifying nouns and not standing alone. If the word is alone, it is a pronoun (see Chapter 6, "Pronouns").

adjective	I did not like *that* movie.
pronoun	I did not like *that*.

adjective	*Three* players sat on the bench.
pronoun	*Three* of the players are injured.

2. **Descriptive adjectives:** A descriptive adjective is any of the thousands of words that describe the people, places, things, and ideas that surround us.

cold	purple	expensive	unusual	massive	deep	honorable
low	fuzzy	liquid	tame	quiet	sharp	unbelievable

Descriptive adjectives are much more flexible than the limiting adjectives. First, they may easily be placed after the noun they modify.

The cave, *deep* and *narrow,* was the perfect hiding place for the thieves.

Also, most of the descriptive adjectives have levels, or grades, called **positive**, **comparative**, and **superlative**. All one-syllable and some two-syllable adjectives add *-er* to form the comparative and add *-est* to form the superlative. A slight spelling change might also have to be made. Other two-syllable adjectives and all adjectives with three or more syllables use the words *more* and *most* or *less* and *least* to form the comparative and superlative.

positive	comparative	superlative
deep	*deeper*	*deepest*
fuzzy	*fuzzier*	*fuzziest*
massive	*more massive*	*most massive*
expensive	*more expensive*	*most expensive*

You should generally use the comparative when comparing two nouns, and the superlative when comparing three nouns or more.

> Your kite is *bigger*, but mine has the *longer* tail.
>
> Of all the posters in the contest, I think yours shows the *best* originality.

Some adjectives have irregular forms. If you are in doubt, check a dictionary.

> *good/better/best*   *well/ better/best*   *bad/worse/worst*   *little/less/least*

Finally, some adjectives do not have comparative or superlative forms. The adjectives *unique* and *perfect*, for example, should be used only in the positive form. Things either are unique or perfect, or they are not.

EXERCISE A: reading for adjectives

Accuracy _____

Directions: Read in a good book and find ten nouns that are preceded by at least one limiting adjective (other than the articles *a, an,* and *the)* and at least one descriptive adjective. Fill in the spaces below with the examples you find. Also tell the title of the book and its author.

Examples:	my first real baseball glove
	the only good choice
	those two plastic bottles

1. _____

2. _____

3. _____

4. _____

5. _____

6. _____

7. _____

8. _____

9. _____

10. _____

Book title and Author: _____

OTHER ADJECTIVE FORMS

1. **Compound adjectives:** Some adjectives are made by combining two or more words with a hyphen. Two-word numbers through ninety-nine are hyphenated, as are fractions used as adjectives. Many compounds are also made from the present participle or past participle forms of verbs.

forty-seven	one hundred *twenty-three*	*two-thirds* majority
high-stepping band	*self-employed* editor	*fur-lined* jacket

2. **Nouns as adjectives:** When a noun precedes another noun to describe it, we call it an adjective.

   ocean breeze   *wool* sweater   *mountain* cabin   *movie* review

   Other such pairings of two nouns have become so common and inseparable that they are considered a single noun unit.

   rain gauge   *tree house*   *vinyl siding*   *lawn mower*

3. **Proper adjectives:** A proper adjective is an adjective formed from a proper noun. Like the proper noun, it is capitalized.

   Japanese economy   *Spanish* poetry   *Hebrew* proverb   *Shakespearean* comedy

4. **Predicate adjective:** Just as a noun or pronoun may follow a linking verb in the predicate, so too may an adjective. It is then called a **predicate adjective**, and it describes the subject.

You must have been *upset* when you found out they had left without you.
Amazingly, the fifth graders remained *quiet* in their seats until the bell rang.

   The linking verbs that may be followed by a predicate adjective are *be, look, sound, taste, feel, smell, appear, remain, grow, prove, turn, seem,* and *become.*

5. **Adjective phrase:** In Chapter 2 you learned about how nouns and prepositions combine to make a prepositional phrase. One of the most important functions of a prepositional phrase is to tell about nouns and pronouns—in other words, to serve as an adjective. A prepositional phrase that functions as an adjective is called an **adjective phrase**.

television *in the living room*	someone *from the principal's office*
Denise *in addition to her brothers*	name *of the band*

ADJECTIVES

Name: _____

EXERCISE B: other adjective forms   **Accuracy** _____ **Creativity** _____

Directions: In this exercise you are to fill in the blanks with adjectives that will modify the noun printed in **bold** type. Use the adjective form that is indicated.

1.   We'll need at least _____**chairs** for the banquet.
                        (compound adjective)

2.   I love stories about_____**villains**.
                        (compound adjective)

3.   My grandmother grew up in _____ **Poland**.
                        (compound adjective)

4.   What is your favorite _____ **sport**?
                        (noun as adjective)

5.   There's a new _____- **show** on television tonight.
                        (noun as adjective)

6.   His father owns a(n) _____ **delivery service**.
                        (noun as adjective)

7.   The storyteller enchanted us with a(n) _____**legend**.
                        (proper adjective)

8.   Have you ever read a(n) _____**novel**?
                        (proper adjective)

9.   For my birthday my parents took me out to a(n) _____**restaurant**.
                        (proper adjective)

10. Our **house** is not very _____ .
                        (predicate adjective)

11. If you ask politely, your **friends** will probably be _____ to let you join.
                        (predicate adjective)

12. My sister tried to keep a straight face, but **Mother** was still _____ .
                        (predicate adjective)

13. Stay away from the **railroad tracks** _____.
                        (adjective phrase)

14. Two **canoes** _____were tied to the roof rack.
                        (adjective phrase)

15. The most popular **poem** _____ was
                        (adjective phrase)

Robert Frost's "Stopping by Woods on a Snowy Evening."

ADJECTIVES

Name: _____

EXERCISE C: adjectives in the sentence

Accuracy _____

Directions: On the line beneath each sentence, write all the adjectives that appear in the sentence. Be sure to include all adjective phrases. Consider an adjective phrase as a single unit, even if it has adjectives within it. You do not have to list the articles.

Use semicolons to separate the adjectives you find. Be prepared to tell what noun or pronoun each adjective is modifying. Notice that you will be graded only on accuracy.

Example: Most of the people in the survey loved these new cookies with toasted marshmallows.
    of the people; in the survey; these; new; with toasted marshmallows   .

1. Most questions on the test required a knowledge of algebra.

    _____

2. With those silly glasses, he looked like Groucho Marx.

    _____

3. Our camp counselor told us a scary story about the river.

    _____

4. The two most popular items on this month's menu are ziti with meat sauce and grilled salmon.

    _____

5. Whose bicycle is that green one in the driveway?

    _____

6. Did any boat at the marina have an aluminum hull?

    _____

7. My new neighbor across the street has an amazing telescope, with a camera and everything.

    _____

8. The answer, plain and simple, is to throw away everything in the attic.

    _____

9. The Norman architecture of the cathedral in Winchester impressed everyone on the tour.

    _____

10. My German friend gave me a menu from the Hofbrau Haus in Munich.

    _____

ADJECTIVES

Name: _____

EXERCISE D: writing with adjectives

Accuracy _____ **Creativity** _____

Directions: Fill in each blank with an adjective of the kind indicated.

Example: <u>*That*</u>   <u>*antique*</u>   table   <u>*on the back porch*</u>   needs
     (*demonstrative*)   (*descriptive*)   (*adjective phrase*)
     <u>*two*</u>   <u>*more*</u>   coats   <u>*of varnish.*</u>
     (*quantifier*)   (*comparative*)   (*adjective phrase*)

1. _____ photograph _____ was _____ .
     (*quantifier*)   (*adjective phrase*)   (*predicate adjective*)

2. _____ idea _____ sounded _____ .
     (*demonstrative*)   (*adjective phrase*)   (*predicate adjective*)

3. _____ _____ jacket is _____ than
     (*possessive*)   (*compound adjective*)   (*descriptive, in comparative*)

   the one _____ .
          (*adjective phrase*)

4. The _____ person _____ will win a(n)
       (*ordinal*)   (*adjective phrase*)

   _____ prize.
      (*descriptive*)

5. I've seen _____ _____ movie, *Minions*, _____ times
        (*possessive*)   (*descriptive*)   (*comparative*)

   than you have, and I still think it is _____ .
           (*predicate adjective*)

6. The _____ acrobat remained _____ , even when
       (*descriptive*)   (*predicate adjective*)

   _____ _____ partner began to shake.
     (*possessive*)   (*descriptive*)

7. _____ animals _____ needed _____ cages.
     (*quantifier*)   (*adjective phrase*)   (*descriptive, in comparative*)

8. The _____ backpack _____ is less _____ than
       (*descriptive*)   (*adjective phrase*)   (*descriptive*)

   the _____ model _____ .
      (*descriptive*)   (*adjective phrase*)

9. I bought the _____ one _____ .
      (*descriptive, in superlative*)   (*adjective phrase*)

10. The_____ puppy, _____ and _____ , licked my hand.
      (*descriptive*)   (*descriptive*)   (*descriptive*)

4. ADVERBS

An adverb is a word or group of words used to modify a verb, an adjective, or another adverb.

Like adjectives, adverbs are called modifiers. They influence or modify the meanings of verbs, adjectives, or other adverbs. Consider this simple sentence.

The dolphins were swimming.

Look at how the meaning of the verb phrase *were swimming* is made more precise or changed by the following adverbs.

slowly   yesterday   gracefully   below   around   not

As you might gather from these samples, adverbs answer a variety of questions about the verbs they are modifying, such as *when?, where?, how?, why?, how much?,* or *under what condition?*

When adverbs are modifying adjectives or other adverbs, they usually are answering the questions *when?, how?,* or *how much?*

slightly scratched   *rarely* angry   *not really* sincere   *very* heavy   *almost fully* grown

Adverbs generally fall into two groups, those that are made from adjectives and those that are not.

1. **Adverbs from adjectives:** Some of the adverbs made from adjectives are exactly the same: *high, low, deep, fast, hard, early, late, much, little, straight, pretty, wrong, fine, enough.*

   Many other adverbs are made by adding *-ly* to an adjective: *quick/quickly, loose/loosely, bad/badly, complete/completely.*

   Be aware of the spelling changes that sometimes have to be made when changing an adjective to an adverb: *angry/angrily, true/truly, sensible/sensibly.*

   Of course, not all words that end in the letters *ly* are adverbs: *sly* (adjective), *fly* (verb or noun), *July* (proper noun).

   Like the adjectives they are made from, adverbs may show the degrees called **positive**, **comparative**, and **superlative**. A few of them are irregular.

positive	comparative	superlative
loud	louder	loudest
frequently	more frequently	most frequently
confidently	more confidently	most confidently
badly	worse	worst
little	less	least
much	more	most
far	farther	farthest
—	further	furthest

2. **Adverbs not from adjectives:** Here is a list of common adverbs not made from adjectives. While the list is not complete, it does give a good indication of the importance and frequency of adverbs.

| **Where?** | here | there | nowhere | somewhere | everywhere | up |
| | south | near | below | home | away | in |

When?	once	twice	today	tomorrow	yesterday	still
	now	forever	never	ever	afterwards	then
	soon	yet	always	often	seldom	before
	daily	yearly	again			

How?	just	very	rather	quite	somewhat	so
or	almost	too	enough	hardly	barely	only
How much?	maybe	perhaps	well	really	undoubtedly	pretty

You will notice that some of these adverbs might also be prepositions (*down, up, near, below,* etc.) or nouns (*today, yesterday, home,* etc.). You can tell the difference by determining what the word is doing in the sentence.

3. **Adverb phrase:** By now you should be quite familiar with the prepositional phrase. It appeared in Chapter 2 to illustrate one of the uses of a noun, as the object of a preposition. Chapter 3 considered its use as an adjective. Now we present the prepositional phrase as an adverb, almost always modifying the verb. It is called the **adverb phrase**. It will answer the same questions as the one-word adverbs.

where?	galloped *into the forest*
when?	slept *during the lecture*
how?	entered *without a sound*
under what condition?	played *in spite of the thunderstorm*

Remember to identify what part of speech a word or a phrase is by determining how it is used in each sentence. The same prepositional phrase might serve as either an adjective phrase or an adverb phrase, depending on its use in the sentence.

| **adjective phrase** | The fence *around the vegetable garden* doesn't keep out rabbits. |
| **adverb phrase** | I mowed *around the vegetable garden,* just as you requested. |

ADVERBS

Name: _____

EXERCISE A: adverbs in the sentence

Accuracy _____

Directions: On the line beneath each sentence, write all the adverbs that appear in the sentence. Be sure to include all adverb phrases. Use semicolons to separate the adverbs you find.

Be prepared to tell what verb, adjective, or adverb each adverb is modifying. Notice that you will be graded only on accuracy.

Example: Immediately after Christmas we again headed south for our annual getaway.
         Immediately; after Christmas; again; south; for our annual getaway

1. With a quick twirl of her fingers, she then spun the pizza dough high into the air.

   _____

2. Before the Thanksgiving dinner the family quietly sat with bowed heads and folded hands.

   _____

3. Quickly, silently, the stage hands worked behind the curtain during the intermission.

   _____

4. Maybe you should just stay home tomorrow.

   _____

5. Every day I walk through the streets like a zombie.

   _____

6. In sheer panic he climbed up onto the roof and yelled for the police.

   _____

7. After the storm, very many people along the coast discovered they had lost nearly everything.

   _____

8. Because of the curfew, we could not stay out on the streets after ten o'clock.

   _____

9. In Paris, almost every restaurant was too expensive for our meager allowance.

   _____

10. The traffic was really much more terrible in Los Angeles than I had expected from your letter.

   _____

EXERCISE B: reading for adjective and adverb phrases   **Accuracy** _____

Directions: This exercise unites the lessons of the last three chapters by focusing on the prepositional phrase and its use as an adjective and an adverb. Read in a good book of fiction and look for ten adjective and ten adverb phrases. Write the phrase itself, followed by the word it modifies. At the bottom, write the name of the book and its author. You may wish to look back at the list of prepositions on pages 17 and 18.

	Adjective phrases	Word modified
1		
2		
3		
4		
5		
6		
7		
8		
9		
10		
	Adverb phrases	**Word modified**
1		
2		
3		
4		
5		
6		
7		
8		
9		
10		
Title + Author:		

ADVERBS

Name: _____

EXERCISE C: writing with adjectives and adverbs

Accuracy _____ **Creativity** _____

Directions: Here is an opportunity to practice using adjectives and adverbs in your own writing. Choose one of the following ideas and write about it on this page and the next.

1.   A time when you had trouble getting something to work
2.   A time when you built or made something for someone else
3.   A time when you had to do something before you were ready

The adjectives will help you describe the setting and the things involved in your activity. The adverbs will tell where and when all this happened, how you went about the action, and the conditions under which it happened.

You may have other people involved in your story, but try to avoid dialogue. Simply keep the focus on the activity itself.

Underline the adjectives and put parentheses around the adverbs.

5. CONJUNCTIONS AND INTERJECTIONS

A conjunction is a word used to join one grammatical construction with another.

In Chapter 2, "Nouns," you learned that two or more nouns may be joined to form multiple noun units called compounds. Other grammatical constructions may also be joined, such as verbs, prepositional phrases, even whole sentences. The part of speech we use to join words or groups of words is called the **conjunction**.

There are four different kinds of conjunctions, but in this chapter we will present only three. Subordinating conjunctions, the fourth kind, are used to construct subordinate clauses, so we will wait until Chapter 8, "Clauses," to present them.

1. **Coordinating conjunctions:** When we want to join sentence parts that are of the same importance, or coordinate, we use a coordinating conjunction. There are seven of them, and it's easy to remember them by the phrase

$$f - a - n - b - o - y - s$$

These letters stand for

for — and — nor — but — or — yet — so

Now look at how the conjunctions are used in these sentences.

I rushed around the house picking up my junk, *for* I knew the guests would soon arrive.

There are seven coordinating conjunctions, *and* I remember them by that silly phrase.

You didn't pick up the broken pieces, *nor* did you even apologize for your clumsiness.

I like the red and blue ones, *but* not the green ones.

I'd love to go to college in New Hampshire *or* Vermont.

They searched for nearly three decades, *yet* they never located their missing aunt.

The holly bush was starting to droop, *so* I transplanted it to a sunnier spot.

When a coordinating conjunction is joining two sentences, it will generally be preceded by a comma. Such a sentence is called a **compound sentence**. Which of the above sentences are compound?

2. **Correlative conjunctions:** These conjunctions travel in pairs.

both...and   either...or   neither...nor   not (only)...but (also)   whether...or

When you use one of these pairs, the two elements they are joining must be of the same grammatical construction.

The weather service reported ***both*** sleet ***and*** hail last night.
                                   (noun)   *(noun)*

You may ***either*** go to the dress rehearsal tonight ***or*** wait for opening night tomorrow.
                (verb)   *(verb)*

I see ads for the new cereal ***not only*** on television ***but also*** in newspapers and magazines.
                  (adverb phrase)   *(adverb phrase)*

3. **Conjunctive adverbs:** These are words that combine the qualities of the conjunction and the adverb. They join sentences, and at the same time they answer the questions of adverbs. The most common conjunctive adverbs are *also, besides, consequently, for example, furthermore, however, in fact, likewise, moreover, nevertheless, otherwise, then, therefore,* and *thus.*

Conjunctive adverbs show a variety of relationships between the sentences they join.

addition	*also, besides, for example, furthermore, in fact, likewise, meanwhile, moreover, then*
contrast	*however, nevertheless, otherwise*
cause and effect	*consequently, therefore, thus*

Be aware of the punctuation you must use with conjunctive adverbs. Write a semicolon before the conjunctive adverb, and usually a comma after it.

You had better arrive before seven o'clock; *otherwise,* you might not get a seat.

The storm had knocked out the electricity; *therefore,* we had no way to cook for two days.

I didn't get to try out my new surfboard; *in fact,* it was so cold that we never left the hotel.

CONJUNCTION ISSUES

1. You must realize that four of the coordinating conjunctions (*for, but, yet, so*) appear as other parts of speech. It is very important not to confuse them. Always look at how these words are used in the sentence.

conjunction	We hurried home, *for* it was starting to rain.
preposition	We wished *for* an umbrella.
conjunction	I called again, *but* no one answered.
preposition	In the refrigerator there was nothing *but* leftovers.
conjunction	I tried as hard as I could, *yet* it was useless.
adverb	Have you finished your math homework *yet?*
conjunction	I knew you wanted to go, *so* I bought an extra ticket.
adverb	The concert was *so* loud that my ears are still ringing.

2. Do not confuse a conjunctive adverb with a simple adverb. A conjunctive adverb must be joining two sentences. Here are some sentences in which the italicized words are simple adverbs.

Sara Donovan, *meanwhile,* made sure the stage crew had all the props.

It was *then* that we realized that we had forgotten to pack the mosquito repellent.

You'll have to buy the batteries and a carrying case *besides.*

CONJUNCTIONS

Name: _____

EXERCISE A: types of conjunctions

Accuracy _____

Directions: Fill in the blanks with appropriate conjunctions. Look back at the lists on the previous two pages, and try to use a different conjunction in each sentence. It will take some planning, for in many cases only one or a few conjunctions will fit the logic and the grammar of the rest of the sentence.

COORDINATING CONJUNCTIONS

1. Would you prefer a cone _____ a dish?

2. We washed our muddy socks _____ then hung them on a tree limb.

3. She had already found a present for her father _____ not for her mother.

4. He wouldn't let us try out for the varsity, _____ could we even stay and watch the practice.

5. There was nothing more to do at the carnival, _____ we just went home.

CORRELATIVE CONJUNCTIONS

6. We could raise the money _____ by selling raffle tickets _____ by collecting returnable bottles and cans.

7. From *Hamlet* comes the famous line "_____ a borrower _____ a lender be."

8. _____ did the airline lose our luggage, _____ we missed our connecting flight to Denver.

9. _____ the tigers _____ the monkeys now have realistic habitats to roam in.

10. We have to decide soon _____ to go out to a movie _____ to rent a video and stay home.

CONJUNCTIVE ADVERBS

11. You stay here and watch the front door; _____ , I'll sneak around back.

12. The battery in my calculator gave out halfway through the test; _____ , I was able to finish before the bell.

13. You simply must do some review during vacation; _____ , you'll never be ready for the final exam.

14. We've had a busy day and there's more to come tomorrow; _____ , I propose we all get a good night's sleep.

15. You can't afford it; _____ , you're not old enough.

CONJUNCTIONS

Name: _____

EXERCISE B: writing with conjunctions

Accuracy _____ **Creativity** _____

Directions: Here we have supplied only the conjunctions and the kinds of items they are to join. You are to write interesting sentences which demonstrate the indicated conjunction function.

1. (*and*, joining two subjects) _____

_____

2. (*or*, joining two indirect objects) _____

_____

3. (*for*, joining two sentences) _____

_____

4. (*yet*, joining two sentences) _____

_____

5. (*not only...but also*, joining two prepositional phrases) _____

_____

6. (*neither...nor*, joining two subjects) _____

_____

7. (*both...and*, joining two direct objects) _____

_____

8. (*however*, joining two sentences) _____

_____

9. (*consequently*, joining two sentences) _____

_____

10. (*nevertheless*, joining two sentences) _____

_____

> **An interjection is a word or group of words used to add a special feeling to a sentence, such as surprise, alarm, excitement, or pleasure.**

Common interjections are *well, oh, ah, ouch, gee, my goodness*, and *boy*. Interjections have no grammatical function in the sentence. They appear much more in speech than in formal writing. Therefore, feel free to use them when you are writing dialogue, but generally avoid them in other writing situations.

INTERJECTIONS

Name: _____

EXERCISE C: writing with interjections

Creativity _____

Directions: Here we have indicated an emotion that might be expressed by using an interjection. Write a sentence for each that begins with an interjection expressing that emotion.

1. (*surprise*) _____

   _____

2. (*alarm*) _____

   _____

3. (*excitement*) _____

   _____

4. (*casualness*) _____

   _____

5. (*pleasure*) _____

   _____

6. PRONOUNS

> **A pronoun is a word used to replace a noun or nouns.**

PERSONAL PRONOUNS

Pronouns give us variety and flexibility in our writing and speaking. If you were writing a history paper about Joan of Arc, you would soon grow tired of calling Joan of Arc by name every time you referred to Joan of Arc (as in this sentence). So instead, you would use a personal pronoun to replace that noun. You would write *she*, *her*, and *hers*, and the reader would still know what noun you meant.

Personal pronouns are the most common pronouns. They may be used in all the ways that a noun may be used. An important difference, however, is that, unlike nouns, they often change their form, or **case**, depending on their use in the sentence. There are three pronoun cases.

1. **Nominative case:** A pronoun must be in the nominative case when it is replacing a subject or a predicate noun. When it replaces a predicate noun, it is often called a **predicate nominative** as a reminder to put it in the nominative case.

subject	*The answers* are in the back of the book. *They* are in the back of the book.
predicate nominative	The caller could not have been *Madeline*. The caller could not have been *she*.

2. **Objective case**: A pronoun is in the objective case when it is replacing a noun that is the direct object, the indirect object, or the object of a preposition.

direct object	I couldn't find *the answers*. I couldn't find *them*.
indirect object	Have you told *Charlie* your new address? Have you told *him* your new address?
object of the preposition	I received a call from *Ellen*. I received a call from *her*.

3. **Possessive case:** The possessive case of pronouns appeared in Chapter 3, "Adjectives," because their usual duty is to modify a noun by telling who owns it. These are called **possessive adjectives**.

> I looked at *Robin's* answers.
> I looked at *her* answers.

Pronouns in the possessive case have more than one form. When both the possessive adjective and the noun it is describing are replaced, we use a possessive pronoun.

> She has *my sweater*.
> She has *mine*.

Here is a summary of the personal pronouns in the three cases.

	Nominative	Objective	Possessive (adjective/pronoun)
Singular			
First person	*I*	*me*	*my/mine*
Second person	*you*	*you*	*your/yours*
Third person	*he*	*him*	*his*
	she	*her*	*her/ hers*
	it	*it*	*its*
Plural			
First person	*we*	*us*	*our/ours*
Second person	*you*	*you*	*your/yours*
Third person	*they*	*them*	*their/theirs*

PRONOUN CASE ISSUES

1. Has anyone ever yelled at you for saying something like, "Him and Dave are coming over tonight"? Probably. And then they tried to give some feeble explanation why it was wrong. And you ended up thinking you could never say "him and Dave" ever again. Right?

    But there's nothing wrong with "him and Dave" if it's in any of the objective case slots.

direct object	Clyde invited *him and Dave* to his house.
indirect object	Clyde gave *him and Dave* a book about magic.
object of preposition	Clyde told all of his secrets to *him and Dave.*

As you might be able to tell from the examples above, the issue of correct case arises most often when a noun and a pronoun are together, or perhaps two pronouns are together. The easiest way to determine the correct case is to take the pronouns one at a time.

He is coming over tonight.
Dave is coming over tonight   = *He and Dave* are coming over tonight.

Clyde showed *him* a new magic trick.
Clyde showed *Dave* a new magic trick.   =   Clyde showed *him and Dave* a new magic trick.

By the way, if you are referring to yourself along with others, courtesy suggests that you put that personal pronoun (*I, me, we, us*) second in the order.

subject	*Dave and I* are going to make him and his dog disappear.
direct object	Clyde invited *Dave and us* to his house.
object of preposition	Clyde told all of his secrets to *Dave and me.*

2. In Chapter 2, "Nouns," you learned about appositives (see page 17). A pronoun may also be an appositive. It must be in the same case as the noun to which it refers, called the **antecedent of the pronoun.**

antecedent and pronoun in nominative case	Only two *people* know for sure, Sarah and *I*.
antecedent and pronoun in objective case	He told just two *people*, Sarah and *me*.

3. One more point before the first exercise. Sometimes we may want to omit a verb in a sentence because it seems to be understood. Without the verb, however, it might be hard to determine the correct case of the pronoun. Mentally supply the missing verb to come up with the correct pronoun. If there is risk of confusion, actually write out the verb.

She likes pepperoni pizza better than *he* (does).
She likes Jasper better than (she likes) *him*.
She likes Jasper better than *he* (likes Jasper).

PRONOUNS

Name: _____

EXERCISE A: personal pronoun use

Accuracy _____ Creativity _____

Directions: In each space, write the correct answer from the choices given. Can any have more than one answer? Use the table on page 44 as a reference.

1. Should I sit between _____ and _____?
    (he/him)   *(she/her)*

2. For _____ and _____ the homework was impossible.
    (I/me/he/him)   *(I/me/he/him)*

3. After all her protests against the bill, I couldn't believe it was _____ who cast the deciding vote for it.
    (she/her)

4. I'm going to invite _____ and his visiting exchange student to the play.
    (he/him)

5. The policeman told _____ and _____ to stay away from the burning car.
    (he/him/I/me)   *(he/him/I/me)*

6. The winner will be _____ who sells the most candy bars.
    (she/her)

7. Only three people received a perfect score on the spelling test—Jackie, Frank, and _____ .
    (I/me)

8. I've been working at this awful job longer than _____ .
    (she/her)

9. After we discussed the science lab, I realized that I understood it even less than _____.
    (she/her)

10. Was your cousin _____ who called at midnight last night?
    (he/him)

11. Have you asked your mother or _____ if they would drive this weekend?
    (she/her)

12. He told the gruesome details only to his closest friends, Charlie and _____ .
    (I/me)

13. I shouldn't have picked on somebody as big as _____.
    (he/him)

14. Why do I get called on so much more often than _____?
    (they/them)

15. Dad bought _____ and _____ ice cream cones after the big game.
    (my friends/I/me)   *(my friends/I/me)*

16. Should _____ or _____ go first?
    (Terry/I/me)   *(Terry/I/me)*

17. Would you like _____ and _____ to bring back some Chinese food?
    (Donna/I/me)   *(Donna/I/me)*

18. No one besides Mother and _____ knew the names of all the players on the field.
    (I/me)

19. Who would make the better class social director, _____ or _____ ?
    (she/her/I/me)   *(she/her/I/me)*

20. I wish that you had told either the nurse or _____ that your foot was still hurting.
    (I/me)

INTERROGATIVE PRONOUNS

Often we do not know a certain person, place, thing, or idea (a certain noun) and we want to find out. So we ask a question, using an **interrogative pronoun**. The pronoun simply substitutes for the noun until we get the real answer. There are only five interrogative pronouns: *who, whose, whom, which*, and *what*.

Who is your lab partner?	*Marcia* is my lab partner.
Whose did you like the best?	I liked *Terry's* the best.
From *whom* did you receive the beautiful flowers?	I received the flowers from *my aunt*.
Which is the home team?	*Detroit* is the home team.
What did you talk about all night?	We talked about *honesty* all night.

DEMONSTRATIVE PRONOUNS

These are easy. A **demonstrative pronoun** is used to point out what noun we are talking about, without saying the noun itself. The first sentence of this paragraph began with a demonstrative pronoun, *these*.

There are four demonstrative pronouns: *this, that, these*, and *those*. They come naturally in our speaking and writing. Just make sure you can determine when these words are being used as pronouns replacing nouns, and when they are being used as adjectives modifying nouns

demonstrative pronoun	*Those* are much too expensive!
adjective	*Those* shoes are much too expensive.

INTENSIVE AND REFLEXIVE PRONOUNS

These are the pronouns: *myself, yourself, himself, herself, itself, ourselves, yourselves*, and *themselves*.

An **intensive pronoun** almost always follows another noun or pronoun and adds emphasis to it.

> The owner of the restaurant *himself* was taking a turn at waiting tables.
> You *yourselves* will have to determine the best way to do the experiment.

A **reflexive pronoun** appears in the predicate of the sentence and, like a reflection in a mirror, refers back to the subject.

> The explorer found *himself* back at his base camp.
> All the costumed creatures helped *themselves* to the Halloween candy.

Do not be tempted to use a reflexive pronoun when you should be using a regular personal pronoun.

Incorrect:	You should talk to Ms. Tillotson or *myself* after lunch.
Correct:	You should talk to Ms. Tillotson or *me* after lunch.

Only *I* can talk to *myself*; *you* can't talk to *myself*, and *I* can't talk to *yourself*. And *I* can't see *yourself* in the mirror!

PRONOUNS

Name: _____

EXERCISE B: interrogative, demonstrative, intensive, and reflexive   **Accuracy** _____

Directions: Fill in the spaces with pronouns as directed. You will be graded only on accuracy.

1. _____ did Vickie _____ order from the catalogue?
    (interrogative)   *(reflexive)*

2. "_____ painted _____?" asked the art teacher.
    (interrogative)   *(demonstrative)*

3. "_____ is how I hurt _____," explained my little brother.
    (demonstrative)   *(intensive)*

4. The presidential candidate _____ led the singing of the National Anthem.
                              (intensive)

5. "_____ did you interview for your biography term paper?"
    (interrogative)

6. "I bought _____ for you and _____ for _____ ."
           (demonstrative)   *(demonstrative)*   *(reflexive)*

7. _____ had more illustrations, hers or yours?
    (interrogative)

8. I _____ have never used either brand of tennis balls, but they tell me _____ are better.
      (intensive)   *(demonstrative)*

9. The ice cream store found _____ unable to keep up with the demand for watermelon sherbet.
                             (reflexive)

10. With _____ did you share the tent on last week's outing club trip?
         (interrogative)

11. You will just have to figure _____ out _____ .
                                (demonstrative)   *(intensive)*

12. _____ was just the news they _____ had hoped for.
    (demonstrative)   *(intensive)*

INDEFINITE PRONOUNS

Imagine that you see *something* moving in the shadows. It must be a person or a thing (that is, a noun), but you can't be any more definite than that. The indefinite pronoun *something* will stand for that person or thing until you can turn on your flashlight and give a definite name to what is actually there.

Indefinite pronouns usually imply some quantity, from none to all. Some of the indefinite pronouns are always singular; some are always plural; and some may be either singular or plural, depending on what they are referring to. Because the verb must agree with the subject in number, it is important for you to be able to determine whether the indefinite pronoun is singular or plural.

Always singular:	*anybody*	*anyone*	*anything*
	everybody	*everyone*	*everything*
	nobody	*no one*	*nothing*
	somebody	*someone*	*something*
	either	*neither*	
	each	*one*	

It is not difficult to see that the pronouns ending in *-body*, *-one*, or *-thing* would be singular or that the word *one* would be singular. For the other three, *either*, *neither*, and *each*, imagine that they are followed by the word *one*, as they often are. That will help you to remember to use the singular verb.

Was either (one) of your answers right?

Neither (one) of my favorite drivers has been in the lead at any time during this race.

Each (one) of the reports on China shows a different aspect of the culture.

Always plural:	*both*	*few*	*many*	*several*

Both of the trails leading down the mountain are blocked by snow drifts.

Only a *few* of the girls *were* willing to volunteer.

Singular or plural:	*all*	*any*	*most*	*none*	*some*

These five indefinite pronouns are usually followed by a stated or implied prepositional phrase beginning with *of.* If the object of the preposition *of* is singular, the verb will be singular. If the object of the preposition *of* is plural, the verb will be plural.

All of the *money was* recovered within three days.

None of the *information* I need about the United Nations *is* in this almanac.

Most of the *dinner is* already on the table.

Do any of your *friends subscribe* to a model trains magazine?

Some of the *graduates are* taking a year off before going to college.

None of the *glasses were* empty.

Another kind of pronoun, the relative pronoun, is used to form an adjective clause and will be presented in Chapter 8.

PRONOUNS

Name: _____

EXERCISE C: indefinite pronouns and verb agreement

Accuracy _____

Directions: Fill in each blank with the correct form of the verb, either singular or plural, based on the indefinite pronoun that is serving as the subject.

1. None of the students caught cheating _____ able to explain why they did it.
    (was) (were)

2. _____ all of the pages have holes punched in them?
    (Does) (Do)

3. All of the volunteers who signed up to go rake leaves tomorrow _____ to be here by eight
    (has) (have)

    o'clock.

4. Some of the best parts of that movie I watched on television last night _____ edited.
    (was) (were)

5. _____ any of the cake been saved for the party this weekend?
    (Has) (Have)

6. Neither of the geography books you recommended _____ an up-to-date map of the African
    (contains) (contain)

    continent.

7. _____ either of the wrenches fit?
    (Does) (Do)

8. Many _____ called but few_____ chosen.
    (is) (are)   *(is) (are)*

9. One of the musicians in the orchestra _____ just composed a symphony.
    (has) (have)

10. Anyone traveling on this flight who needs assistance with boarding the airplane _____ asked to
    (is) (are)

    come to the front of the line now.

OTHER PRONOUN ISSUES

When you use a pronoun, remember that it is substituting for a noun or another pronoun, called its **antecedent**. The antecedent of a pronoun must be clear, or the sentence will be confusing. For each of the examples below, we offer one way to make the sentence clear. Can you think of other ways?

Unclear:	Charlie brought home a pet snake, and Dad said *he* would have to sleep in the back hall.
Clear:	Charlie brought home a pet snake, and Dad said, *"That snake* will have to sleep in the back hall."

Unclear:	I handed the baby back to my sister and then gave *her* the rattle.
Clear:	I handed the baby back to my sister and then gave *my sister* the rattle.

Unclear:	The teachers told the students that *they* were feeling disappointed.
Clear:	The teachers told the students, *"We* are feeling disappointed."

Unclear:	When I saw the whipped cream on your pudding, I decided to order *it,* too.
Clear:	When I saw the whipped cream on your pudding, I decided to order *some pudding,* too.

Also, avoid an awkward reference back to an antecedent in the possessive case.

Unclear:	In my sister's book bag she always keeps a peanut butter sandwich.
Clear:	My sister always keeps a peanut butter sandwich in her book bag.

And finally, make sure that there is an antecedent for the pronoun to refer to.

Unclear:	As an amateur artist, I spent all day painting the beautiful oak tree in my backyard, and now I'm going to put *it* in my room.
Clear:	As an amateur artist, I spent all day painting the beautiful oak tree in my back yard, and now I'm going to put *the painting* in my room.

PRONOUNS

Name: _____

EXERCISE D: correcting pronouns errors

Accuracy _____

Directions: Each sentence below has some form of pronoun error in it. You should rewrite the entire sentence so that the meaning will be clear. There may be more than one correct answer.

1. Cindy asked Michelle whether she could baby-sit for her little sister.

   _____

2. Before I could get to the telephone, it had stopped.

   _____

3. My uncle has a golden retriever puppy, and he's losing his teeth.

   _____

4. With Phil's new shortwave radio he can pick up soccer games in Argentina.

   _____

5. Just call Jean Hamilton or myself if you have any questions.

   _____

6. I took the headphones off my ears, and now I can't find them.

   _____

7. If the battery ever leaks in this flashlight, we'll give you a new one.

   _____

8. I love to write, but nobody ever likes it.

   _____

9. Jill and myself never got to the top of the hill.

   _____

10. When the patient entered the doctor's office, she looked frightened.

    _____

7. PHRASES

A phrase is a group of related words that does not contain a subject and a verb. A phrase usually acts as a single part of speech.

By now you have heard the term **phrase** on several occasions. A **verb phrase** was the main verb plus any helping verbs. A **prepositional phrase** was a preposition plus an object of that preposition. It should be easy to apply the definition above to the phrases you have already learned. A verb phrase, of course, acts as a verb, and a prepositional phrase acts as either an adjective or an adverb.

In this chapter we will present four additional phrases, all made directly from verbs: the **infinitive phrase**, the **gerund phrase**, the **present participial phrase**, and the **past participial phrase**. Because these phrases are made from verbs, they are often called **verbals**.

INFINITIVE PHRASE

You probably remember that the infinitive verb form is used to give a command (imperative) as well as to create the present tense of most verbs. By adding the word *to* before the infinitive form, we create a grammatical unit that may be used in a variety of ways: as a noun, as an adjective, or as an adverb. An infinitive often has an object and various modifiers, and together they form an **infinitive phrase**.

1. **Infinitive phrase as noun:** Here are four examples showing how an infinitive phrase can function as a noun in the sentence.

subject	*To win the lottery* is the dream of some people.
direct object	We wanted *to surprise her.*
object of the preposition	The rebels had no choice but *to give up.*
predicate noun	The secret was *to get there five minutes early.*

    Sometimes the infinitive will appear without the word *to.*

    > He said he'd do anything except [*to*] *wash windows.*

2. **Infinitive phrase as adjective:** Sometimes (not very often) an infinitive phrase will be used as an adjective. It will follow the noun or pronoun it is modifying.

This is a wonderful place *to have a picnic.*	**modifies *place***
Everything *to send to the shelter* had been loaded into the van.	**modifies *Everything***

3. **Infinitive phrase as adverb:** The most common use of the infinitive phrase is as an adverb, telling *why* a verb happened. (Remember the chicken crossing the road?) It may appear in different places in the sentence.

To get a better look, I stood on a milk crate.	**modifies *stood***
My sister, *to get back at me,* let the air out of my tires.	**modifies *let***
They arrived at the concert an hour early *to get a good seat.*	**modifies *arrived***

As an adverb, an infinitive phrase may also modify an adjective.

We were all happy *to get home.*	**modifies *happy***

THE INFINITIVE PHRASE: SAMPLES

To watch my boy go off to school alone made me wonder where the days had gone.

—Shirley Jackson, "Charles"

They did not like *to think of their sick comrades in the hands of human beings.*

—George Orwell, *Animal Farm*

There comes a time in every rightly constructed boy's life when he has a raging desire *to go somewhere and dig for hidden treasure.*

—Mark Twain, *Tom Sawyer*

To get [the hundred-dollar bill] changed in a lodging house would be *to take his life in his hands*—he would almost certainly be robbed, and perhaps murdered, before morning.

—Upton Sinclair, *The Jungle*

To get hold of him, she had had to arm herself with a whitethorn branch and sit in the aloe hills above the nest of the wild ostrich pair for days until she had finally managed *to steal three chicks to bring home.*

—Darlene Matthee, *Fiela's Child*

PHRASES

Name: _____

EXERCISE A: infinitive phrases

Accuracy _____ Creativity _____

Directions: Fill in the spaces below with infinitive phrases of your own construction. The function of the infinitive phrase in the sentence is indicated below each space.

1. _____ took over an hour.
    (subject)

2. _____ will cost as much.
    (subject)

3. _____ will get you nowhere.
    (subject)

4. _____ meant we could reduce
    (subject)
our travel time by twenty minutes.

5. Did you attempt _____ ?
    (direct object)

6. She hesitated _____ but not
    (direct object)
_____ .

7. I have decided _____
    (direct object)

8. Up till now I have never needed _____ .
    (direct object)

9. I never expected _____ .
    (direct object)

10. The hardest part of the job will be _____
     (predicate noun)
_____ .

11. My top priority was _____ .
     (predicate noun)

12. Our challenge is _____
     (predicate noun)
_____ on time.

13. The most likely candidate _____
                                (adjective modifying **candidate***)*

_____ is the incumbent.

14. Her effort _____ was unsuccessful.
                   (adjective modifying **effort***)*

15. I appreciated your attempt _____ .
                             (adjective modifying **attempt***)*

16. Were you able _____
                      (adverb modifying **able***)*

_____ ?

17. I was determined _____
                      (adverb modifying **determined***)*

_____ .

18. The worker dug a hole _____ .
                      (adverb modifying **dug***)*

19. _____ , I needed help.
                      (adverb modifying **needed***)*

20. He went back home _____ .
                      (adverb modifying **went***)*

EXERCISE B: reading for infinitive phrases　　　　　　　　**Accuracy** _____

Directions: Read in a good book and find three sentences containing infinitive phrases. Write out the sentences below. Put parentheses around each phrase, and be able to tell the function of the phrase in the sentence. Is it a noun, an adjective, or an adverb? Also tell the title of the book and its author.

_____

_____

_____

_____

_____

_____

_____

_____

_____

Book title: _____

Author: _____

GERUND PHRASE

Recall now the principal part of the verb called the present participle, the one that always ends in *-ing*. When this verb form changes to a noun in a sentence, it is called a **gerund**. Look at the examples.

start with the main verb	I was *surfing.*
gerund as subject	*Surfing* takes great agility.
gerund as direct object	I practiced *surfing.*
gerund as object of the preposition	I impressed my friends by *surfing.*
gerund as predicate noun	My favorite sport is *surfing.*

Like the infinitive, a gerund may have an object and various modifiers. In such a case we have a **gerund phrase**. Consider these examples:

main verb + direct object + modifier	I was *mowing the lawn yesterday.*
gerund phrase as subject	*Mowing the lawn yesterday* took over an hour.
gerund phrase as direct object	I hated *mowing the lawn yesterday.*
gerund phrase as object of the preposition	I earned ten dollars by *mowing the lawn yesterday.*
gerund phrase as predicate noun	My biggest chore was *mowing the lawn yesterday.*

main verb + modifiers	I was *writing on both sides of the paper.*
gerund phrase as subject	*Writing on both sides of the paper* saved at least one twig from a tree.
gerund phrase as direct object	The teacher discouraged *writing on both sides of the paper.*
gerund phrase as object of the preposition	How do you feel about *writing on both sides of the paper?*
gerund phrase as predicate noun	My favorite way of annoying a teacher is *writing on both sides of the paper.*

THE GERUND PHRASE: SAMPLES

And thus the first step to *finding Margaret Billy Sosi* was *finding Hosteen Joseph Joe and asking him the question Sharkey hadn't asked,* which was what Albert Gorman had said to him at the Shiprock Economy Wash-O-Mat.

—Tony Hillerman, *The Ghostway*

But Ducely, who was in the habit of *dousing his plate with chocolate sauce in quantities that sickened the others,* paused in the act of *reaching for the sauce.*

—Herman Wouk, *The Caine Mutiny*

He realized that it was no longer a mere matter of *freezing his fingers.*

—Jack London, *The Call of the Wild*

I risked *inflaming Judith's rage* by *remarking that it would be more sensible to find some drug that would counteract the aftereffects of measles*!

—Agatha Christie, *Curtain*

Eventually, after a week or two of this sneaking sort of life, by *watching and following the guards and taking what chances he could,* he managed to find out where each dwarf was kept.

—J.R.R. Tolkien, *The Hobbit*

Being married to an old army man and the daughter of another had made her a prompt and efficient packer.

—Nicholas Meyer, *The Seven-Per-Cent Solution*

In Muldoon's opinion, *cloning dinosaurs in a laboratory* was one thing. *Maintaining them in the wild* was quite another.

—Michael Crichton, *Jurassic Park*

(Use the space below for **Exercise D**, page 60.)

PHRASES

Name: _____

EXERCISE C: gerund phrases

Accuracy _____ **Creativity** _____

Directions: Fill in the spaces below with gerund phrases of your own construction. The function of the gerund phrase in the sentence is indicated below each space.

1. _____ was the most difficult
    (subject)

    thing she ever had to do.

2. _____ took a lot of courage.
    (subject)

3. _____ will help you feel better.
    (subject)

4. _____ made him look silly.
    (subject)

5. _____ upset the other
    (subject)

    members of the team.

6. I have always loved _____
    (direct object)

    _____ .

7. Have you ever tried _____ ?
    (direct object)

8. She enjoys _____ but not
    (direct object)

    _____ .
    (direct object)

9. All night long I kept _____ .
    (direct object)

10. Suddenly I remembered _____
    (direct object)

    _____ .

11. Did you have anything to do with _____ ?
    (object of the preposition)

12. By _____ ,
$$\quad$$ *(object of the preposition)*

we earned enough money to hire a professional disc jockey.

13. Instead of _____ , they went home .
$$\quad$$ *(object of the preposition)*

14. I have nothing against _____ .
$$\quad$$ *(object of the preposition)*

15. Since _____ , I've been sick .
$$\quad$$ *(object of the preposition)*

16. The hardest part of her new job is _____ .
$$\quad$$ *(predicate noun)*

_____ .

17. The first order of business is _____ .
$$\quad$$ *(predicate noun)*

18. My first objective was _____
$$\quad$$ *(predicate noun)*

_____ before midnight .

19. The scariest moment must have been _____
$$\quad$$ *(predicate noun)*

_____ .

20. Her favorite pastime was _____ .
$$\quad$$ *(predicate noun)*

EXERCISE D: reading for gerund phrases $\qquad$ Accuracy _____

Directions: Read in a good book and find three sentences containing gerund phrases. Write out the sentences on Page 58, or on one of the blank pages elsewhere in the book. Put parentheses around each phrase, and be able to tell the function of the phrase in the sentence. Also tell the title of the book and its author, below.

Book title: _____

Author: _____

PRESENT PARTICIPIAL PHRASE

To make a gerund, we took the present participle form of the verb and used it as a noun. We may also take the present participle form of the verb and use it as an adjective.

main verb	The dog was *barking*.
present participle modifier	The *barking* dog probably had fleas.

Like the gerund and the infinitive, the present participle begins its life as a main verb in a sentence, along with a direct object and various modifiers.

The burning warehouse was *spewing black smoke across the valley*.

(main verb *spewing*) + (object *black smoke*) + (modifier *across the valley*)

When we remove the phrase from the original sentence, we call it a **present participial phrase**. We can then take the entire phrase and add it to another sentence, using it as a nice, fancy adjective.

original sentence	The burning warehouse was *spewing black smoke across the valley*.
another related sentence	The burning warehouse could be seen for miles.
sentences combined	*Spewing black smoke across the valley*, the burning warehouse could be seen for miles.

We have taken two sentences and made them into one. The present participial phrase *spewing black smoke across the valley* performs an adjective function, modifying *the burning warehouse*. Of course, the modifier *burning* is also a present participle, similar to *barking* in the example above.

Present participial phrases often may be placed at several locations in the sentence.

The burning warehouse, *spewing black smoke across the valley*, could be seen for miles.

The burning warehouse could be seen for miles, *spewing black smoke across the valley*.

Be careful, however, that the phrase really is modifying what you want it to.

Incorrect: *Spewing black smoke across the valley,* we could see the burning warehouse.

(*We* were not *spewing black smoke across the valley!*)

Note: Because a gerund phrase and a present participial phrase look exactly alike, they are easy to confuse. Always look at how a word or words are used in a sentence. Remember that a gerund phrase is a noun and a present participial phrase is an adjective.

THE PRESENT PARTICIPIAL PHRASE: SAMPLES

Anticipating that I would try to run, Annie tied me up.

—Stephen King, *Misery*

My parents stand in their back yard, hands on their hips, *looking over the expanse of raw mud, planning their garden.*

—Margaret Atwood, *Cat's Eye*

Hastily flinging her cloak around her, she opened the door and followed, *putting out the candles as if she were never coming back.*

—Thomas Hardy, *Tess of the D'Urbervilles*

This was the Dark, *rising, rising to swallow Will Stanton before he could grow strong enough to do it harm.*

—Susan Cooper, *The Dark Is Rising*

Then they swam on ahead of the canoe, *crossing back and forth in front of it, diving in and out,* as if they were weaving a piece of cloth with their broad snouts.

—Scott O'Dell, *Island of the Blue Dolphins*

We stood there, *squeezing each other's hand to the point of pain.*

—Katherine Paterson, *Jacob Have I Loved*

(Use the space below, or one of the blank pages elsewhere in the book, for **Exercise F**, page 64.)

PHRASES

Name: _____

EXERCISE E: present participial phrases

Accuracy _____

Directions: In this exercise, combine the two given sentences by forming a present participial phrase from the first one and adding it to the second one. You may be able to place the phrase in more than one location, but be sure it modifies the appropriate noun.

Example: Dennis was trying out his new skateboard.
Dennis twisted his ankle and scraped both knees.

Trying out his new skateboard, Dennis twisted his ankle and scraped both knees.

1. I was reading about my family's genealogy.
I discovered that I am related to a famous poet.

_____

_____

2. The fireworks were exploding high over our heads.
The fireworks looked dazzling.

_____

_____

3. She had been noticing smoke coming from the starboard engine.
She pushed the button for the flight attendant.

_____

_____

4. I was lying in the big leather recliner.
I was gently brushing the cat.

_____

_____

5. The old woman was feeding the swans.
The old woman stood at the edge of the water.

_____

_____

6. The baby was crying in the next room.
   The baby distracted the parents at the recital.

   _____

   _____

7. The doctor was holding the tweezers like a teacup.
   The doctor gently pulled out the splinter.

   _____

   _____

8. The mate was untying the bowline from the cleat.
   The mate cast us off from the dock.

   _____

   _____

9. My father was trying to find our location on the map.
   My father sat by the side of the road.

   _____

   _____

10. The policeman was motioning to the first car.
    The policeman directed the line of traffic around the accident.

    _____

    _____

EXERCISE F: reading for present participial phrases   **Accuracy** _____

Directions: Read in a good book and find three examples of present participial phrases. Write out the sentences below, or on Page 62, or on one of the blank pages elsewhere in the book. Put parentheses around each phrase. Also tell the title of the book and its author. (Can you find all three in one sentence?)

_____

_____

_____

_____

Book title: _____

Author: _____

PHRASES

Name: _____

EXERCISE G: writing present participial phrases

Accuracy _____ Creativity _____

Directions: In this exercise, we have supplied only part of the final sentence. You are to add present participial phrases of your own creation that tell more about the nouns or pronouns printed in **bold** type.

> **Example:** Every **fish** _____*measuring less than seven inches*_____ should be thrown back.

1. _____ ,

   we began watching the video we had downloaded.

2. **Everyone** _____

   _____ will need to bring a lunch.

3. The **smells**_____

   _____ brought back memories of my childhood.

4. I just looked at **her** _____

   _____ .

5. My little **brother,** _____

   _____ , started to cry.

6. Not _____ ,

   we just got more frustrated.

7. _____

   _____ , **she** walked home.

8. **He** spent forever in front of the mirror, _____

   _____ and

   _____ .

9. _____

   _____ , the **candidate** tried to go back on her word.

10. The **lights** _____

    _____ began to hypnotize me.

11. _____ but not

_____ , **I** went to my desk and sat down.

12. **Most** of the spectators _____

were cheering for the other team.

13. **We** searched almost two hours for the art museum, _____

_____ and then

_____ .

14. _____ and

_____ , the **alligator** disappeared from view.

15. _____ ,

I suddenly realized that I was too late.

16. The **mechanic** tried for over an hour to get the car started, first _____

_____ and then

_____ .

17. **Anyone** not _____ will have to leave.

18. The **server** at our table, _____

_____ , began to clear our plates.

19. **I** cried, _____

_____ .

20. **Everyone** had a great time, _____ ,

_____ , and

_____ .

PAST PARTICIPIAL PHRASE

Another principal part of a verb, you remember, is the past participle. Like the present participle, it may be used as an adjective.

main verb	The kitten had been *abandoned.*
past participle modifier	The *abandoned* kitten eagerly drank the milk.

As with other phrases, the past participle may have its own modifiers, making it a **past participial phrase**. It will not have an object, however, since the action of the participle is being done to the subject rather than to a direct object.

Over three hundred citizens have been *left homeless by the floods.*

(main verb *left)* + (adverb *homeless*) + (modifier *by the floods)*

We may take the phrase from the original sentence and use it as an adjective.

original sentence	Over three hundred citizens have been *left homeless by the floods.*
another related sentence	Over three hundred citizens crowded into the shelter.
sentences combined	Over three hundred citizens *left homeless by the floods* crowded into the shelter.

Like the present participial phrase, the past participial phrase may often be placed in various locations in the sentence. Make sure, again, that you are modifying the correct noun or pronoun.

Incorrect: *Left homeless by the floods,* we welcomed over three hundred citizens to the shelter.

We (let us hope) were not *left homeless by the floods.*

THE PAST PARTICIPIAL PHRASE: SAMPLES

Betrayed by his stomach, Piggy threw a picked bone down on the beach and stooped for more.

—William Golding, *Lord of the Flies*

The water, *touched to gold by the early sun*, the brooding mists under the banks at some distance down the stream, the fort, the soldiers, the piece of drift—all had distracted him.

—Ambrose Bierce, "An Occurrence at Owl Creek Bridge"

Across the floor Maggie sailed like a coquettish yacht *convoyed by a stately cruiser*.

—O. Henry, "The Coming Out of Maggie"

So when Gilon's turn came to give Omry a present, Omry was very surprised when a large parcel was put before him, *untidily wrapped in brown paper and a string*.

—Lynne Reid Banks, *The Indian in the Cupboard*

Today, *surrounded by thirty interested children under twelve and forty uninterested sheep under five*, she was teaching an important item on the curriculum: the Naming of Rules.

—Ursula Le Guin, "The Naming of Rules"

His face was of a good open expression, but *sunburnt very dark, and heavily freckled and pitted with the smallpox*.

—Robert Lewis Stevenson, *Kidnapped*

She had sort of oaky hair that the sun and salt had bleached, *done up in a bun that was unravelling*, and a kind of prim face.

—John Updike, "A & P"

PHRASES

EXERCISE H: past participial phrases

Name: _____

Accuracy _____ Creativity _____

Directions: In this exercise, combine the two given sentences by forming a past participial phrase from the first one and adding it to the second one. You may be able to place the phrase in more than one location, but be sure it modifies the appropriate noun.

Example: My mother was very concerned about our dog's constant scratching.
My mother called the vet.

Very concerned about our dog's constant scratching, my mother called the vet.

1. The tree was beautifully decorated and lit with little white lights.
The tree made a festive backdrop for the party.

    _____

    _____

2. The piñata was hung from the elm tree.
The blindfolded birthday girl swung furiously at the piñata.

    _____

    _____

3. Those steaks had been broiled over a hickory fire.
Those steaks were delicious.

    _____

    _____

4. The canoe had been made entirely by hand.
The canoe was a true work of art.

    _____

    _____

5. Some at the Halloween party will be dressed as cartoon characters.
People at the Halloween party will get a prize.

    _____

    _____

6. The pages had been torn from the notebook.
The pages lay scattered over the playground.

    _____

    _____

7. I was dismayed by the attitude of the teachers toward the homework.
   I wrote to the principal.

   _____

   _____

8. The items were bought at the going-out-of-business sale.
   None of the items were returnable.

   _____

   _____

9. The boy was frustrated by the unwillingness of the fish to cooperate.
   The boy sat on the end of the pier.

   _____

   _____

10. The marshmallow had been burnt beyond recognition.
    Ted stared at the marshmallow on the end of his stick.

    _____

    _____

EXERCISE I: reading for past participial phrases   **Accuracy** _____

Directions: Read in a good book and find three examples of past participial phrases. Write out the sentences below. Put parentheses around each phrase. Also tell the title of the book and its author.

_____

_____

_____

_____

_____

_____

_____

Book title: _____

Author: _____

PHRASES

EXERCISE J: writing past participial phrases

Name: _____

Accuracy _____ Creativity _____

Directions: In this exercise, we have supplied only part of the final sentence. You are to add past participial phrases of your own creation which tell more about the nouns or pronouns printed in **bold** type.

Example: *Disappointed with store-bought tomato sauces*, Charles decided to make his own.

1. _____

   _____ , **we** got the surprise of our lives.

2. The **hot dogs** _____

   tasted better than the **hot dogs** _____ .

3. The **quarterback** sat on the bench, thoroughly _____ .

4. Most of the **items** _____ were new.

5. _____

   _____ , the old **car** just wasn't worth repairing.

6. The **Pilgrims**, _____

   _____ , sailed in search of a new country where they could have religious freedom.

7. _____

   _____ , my **dog** dug his way under the fence.

8. The prison **cell**, _____

   _____ , offered no hope of escape.

9. There was only a tiny **piece** remaining, _____ and

   _____ .

10. **Nobody** _____

    _____ should do it.

_____

11. _____

_____ , **I** could only look on with awe.

12. Most of the tropical **fish** _____

_____ originated from the Great Barrier Reef off Australia.

13. My favorite old **sweater**, _____

_____ , finally had to be thrown out.

14. The little **children**, _____ ,

came running in to dry.

15. _____ ,

the marathon **runner** had to drop out of the race.

16. Most **people** _____

_____ will just hang up the phone.

17. **I** packed my suitcase, _____

_____ .

18. **Anyone** _____

_____ will have to fill out a report.

19. My English **teacher**, _____

_____ , acted out both parts of the balcony scene from *Romeo and Juliet*.

20. The little **village**, _____

_____ , was the perfect location for filming the movie.

8. CLAUSES

> **A clause is a group of related words that contains a subject and a verb.**

INDEPENDENT AND DEPENDENT CLAUSES

Up to this point, you have been studying the **independent clause,** a group of words that contains a subject and a verb and is able to stand by itself and express a complete thought.

Independent clauses	Mother carefully slid the turkey into the oven.
	This book needs more pictures.
	The building suddenly began to shake.

In this chapter we will look at another kind of clause, the **dependent clause**, sometimes known as a **subordinate clause**. It also has a subject and a verb, but it is not able to stand by itself. It depends on additional words to make sense. Look at the following groups of words. All of them have a subject and a verb, but they do not make sense by themselves.

Dependent clauses	as soon as the swimming pool was filled
	which I keep under my bed
	that my grandparents would be arriving tomorrow

It is easy to take each of the dependent clauses and create a logical sentence.

As soon as the swimming pool was filled, we put on our bathing suits and dived in.
Would you like to see the things *which I keep under my bed*?
I didn't know *that my grandparents would be arriving tomorrow.*

There are three kinds of dependent clauses: adverb, adjective, and noun.

ADVERB CLAUSE

You have studied the adverb in several forms so far: the single word, the prepositional phrase, and the infinitive phrase. An adverb may also be in the form of a clause. Like all clauses, it will contain a subject and a verb, but it also contains something extra: a **subordinating conjunction**.

A subordinating conjunction is a word (or two or three) that allows an independent clause to be joined to another sentence or sentence part. Here are the subordinating conjunctions that help create an adverb clause.

after	although	as	because	before	if
lest	once	since	than	though	till
unless	until	when(ever)	where(ever)	whereas	while
as if	as soon as	as though	even if	even though	
in case	in order that	provided that	so that		

Most adverb clauses are made by taking one of the subordinating conjunctions and adding it to an independent clause. Like adverbs, adverb clauses answer a variety of questions: *when?, how?, why?, how much?,* or *under what condition?*

before	+	the runner reached second base
unless	+	she memorizes her lines by Thursday
even though	+	I paid for it with my own money

ADVERB CLAUSE ISSUES

1. There are several words on the list of subordinating conjunctions that also appear on the list of prepositions. Notice that they all refer to time: *after, as, before, since, till, until.*

   Functioning as a preposition, each of these words is followed by a noun, the **object of the preposition**.

   > The tickets were sold out *before noon.*
   > I'm not leaving *until tomorrow.*

   Functioning as a subordinating conjunction, each of these words is followed by a clause, which means that there must be a subject and a verb.

   > The tickets were sold out *before we arrived at the box office.*
   > I'm not leaving *until I have seen the pandas.*

2. On the list of subordinating conjunctions, you see *as soon as.* Actually, almost any adverb or adjective may be used in this phrase to introduce an adverb clause. Think about clauses that could begin with *as long as, as fast as, as far as, as big as,* or *as tired as.*

THE ADVERB CLAUSE: SAMPLES

Because so much of the ritual had been forgotten or discarded, Mr. Summers had been successful in having slips of paper substituted for the chips of wood that had been used for generations.

—Shirley Jackson "The Lottery"

Before he reached the corner, however, he slowed *as if a wind had sprung up from nowhere, as if someone had called his name.*

—Ray Bradbury, *Fahrenheit 451*

So although she never seemed to urge me to talk, I began to do so, *until, finally, I was pouring out my anguish, not for the cats, but for myself as a murderer.*

—Katherine Paterson, *Jacob Have I Loved*

When the ham boiling had cooled, he filled Sounder's pan and ran his fingers up and down the great dog's back *as he lapped it up.*

—William H. Armstrong, *Sounder*

In hostile silence, the girls stared out of opposite windows *until the cab pulled up in front of Selena's apartment house.*

—J. D. Salinger, "Just Before the War with the Eskimos"

Before he had gone fifty yards, Angeline had overtaken him and, *while I am not prepared to swear to this,* I had the distinct impression that she somehow tripped him.

—Farley Mowat, *Never Cry Wolf*

If she had gone untidy, made grotesque faces, given jerks and starts and twitches, if she had in some way lost their respect, I do not think she would have lost their approval.

—Muriel Spark, "Come Along, Marjorie"

As soon as he closed the door behind him, Phule puffed out his cheeks in a long exhale *as if he had been holding his breath.*

—Robert Asprin, *Phule's Company*

CLAUSES

Name: _____

EXERCISE A: writing adverb clauses

Accuracy _____ Creativity _____

Directions: In each number below, we have provided an independent clause. From the list of subordinating conjunctions, select one that could turn the independent clause into an adverb clause. Then finish the sentence with a new independent clause that makes sense with the rest of the material.

after	although	as	because	before	if
lest	once	since	than	though	till
unless	until	when(ever)	where(ever)	whereas	while
as if	as soon as	as though	even if	even though	
in case	in order that	provided that	so that		

Examples: _Although_   I had tried not to make a sound,   _I still woke up my parents._
                    (conjunction)   *(independent clause)*

She hurried back to her car   _before_   the meter expired.
(independent clause)   *(conjunction)*

1. _____ I couldn't get my locker unlocked, _____ .
   (conjunction)   *(independent clause)*

2. _____ the apartment building will have to be demolished, _____
   (conjunction)   *(independent clause)*

   _____ .

3. _____ the comet was discovered three years ago, _____
   (conjunction)   *(independent clause)*

   _____ .

4. _____
   (independent clause)

   _____ _____ you get your act together.
                                                (conjunction)

5. _____
   (independent clause)

   _____ , _____ he knew I was not telling the truth.
                                                 (conjunction)

6. _____ we didn't have enough money, _____
   (conjunction)   *(independent clause)*

   _____ .

7. _____ you ask your parents' permission, _____
   (conjunction)   *(independent clause)*

   _____ .

8. _____
   (independent clause)

   _____ , _____ the wrestling coach demonstrated a takedown.
   (conjunction)

9. _____ he arrived before I did, _____ .
   (conjunction)   *(independent clause)*

10. _____ my sister worked in Hollywood, _____
    (conjunction)   *(independent clause)*

    _____ .

11. _____ _____ we hurt ourselves.
    (independent clause)   *(conjunction)*

12. _____ she tried as hard as she could, _____
    (conjunction)   *(independent clause)*

    _____ .

13. _____ those stories about UFOs are true, _____
    (conjunction)   *(independent clause)*

    _____ .

14. _____ , _____ they looked everywhere, _____
    (subject of independent clause)   *(conjunction)*   *(predicate of independent clause)*

    _____ .

15. _____ _____ I had anticipated.
    (independent clause)   *(conjunction)*

16. _____ the diet worked for me, _____
    (conjunction)   *(independent clause)*

    _____ .

17. _____
    (independent clause)

    _____ _____ the doctor might determine the cause of the problem.
                                           (conjunction)

18. _____
    (independent clause)

    _____ _____ we become separated.
                                       (conjunction)

19. _____ the sophomores had finished washing the cars, _____
    (conjunction)   *(independent clause)*

    _____ .

20. _____
    (independent clause)

    _____ _____ we get there on time.
                                       (conjunction)

CLAUSES

Name: _____

EXERCISE B: reading for adverb clauses

Accuracy _____

Directions: Now, read in a good book and find three sentences containing adverb clauses. You will probably find them more quickly in your history or science book rather than in a work of fiction. Write out the sentences below, putting parentheses around each clause. Also tell the title of the book and its author.

_____

_____

_____

_____

_____

_____

_____

_____

_____

_____

_____

_____

_____

_____

_____

_____

Book title: _____

Author: _____

ADJECTIVE CLAUSE

The second kind of dependent clause is the **adjective clause**, and it is an easy way to combine sentences that have a noun or pronoun in common.

Sentence A	*The attorney* did not have his facts straight.
Sentence B	*The attorney* prosecuted the case.

You know from your study of personal pronouns that we could use *he* to replace one of the repeated subject nouns. But we would still have two sentences.

To create an adjective clause, we use a different category of pronouns, the **relative pronouns**: *who, whose, whom, which,* and *that.*

Sometimes, when the noun refers to place, time, or reason, we replace it with a **relative adverb**: *where, when,* or *why.* These usually sound more natural and less formal than *in which* or *for which.*

Here is how we join those two sentences, using a relative pronoun. First we strike out the repeated noun, then we replace it with the appropriate relative pronoun.

Sentence A	*The attorney* did not have his facts straight.
Sentence B	~~*The attorney*~~ prosecuted the case.
Relative pronoun	*who*
Final sentence	The attorney *who prosecuted the case* did not have his facts straight.

The adjective clause is *who prosecuted the case.* The subject of the adjective clause is the relative pronoun *who,* and the verb is *prosecuted.*

An adjective clause is sometimes called a **relative clause**. The relative pronoun or relative adverb is related to a noun or pronoun, called the **antecedent**, which has already been mentioned in the sentence. In our example, the antecedent would be *the attorney.*

Here is how to use the other relative pronouns and a relative adverb. Be able to identify the subject and verb of each adjective clause.

Sentence A	We handed out the first questionnaire to *the applicants.*
Sentence B	~~*The applicants'*~~ names began with *A* through *J.*
Relative pronoun	*whose*
Final sentence	We handed out the first questionnaire to the applicants *whose names began with* A *through* J.

Sentence A	*Every person* was from out of state.
Sentence B	We met ~~*every person*~~.
Relative pronoun	*whom*
Final sentence	Every person *whom we met* was from out of state.

Sentence A	Was *the marker* permanent?
Sentence B	You used ~~*the marker*~~ on your Halloween costume.
Relative pronoun	*which* (or *that*)
Final sentence	Was the marker *which you used on your Halloween costume* permanent?

Sentence A	*The stadium* is going to be renovated.
Sentence B	The Orioles' farm team plays ~~*in the stadium*~~.
Relative adverb	*where*
Final sentence	The stadium *where the Orioles' farm team plays* is going to be renovated.

ADJECTIVE CLAUSE ISSUES

1. Like the appositive (see page 17), the adjective clause is sometimes set off from the rest of the sentence with commas, and other times it is not. If the information contained in the clause is essential in order to know which noun or pronoun is intended, we do not use commas. If the information is not essential, because the noun or pronoun is clear from the rest of the sentence, we use commas.

    Here are some examples of sentences containing adjective clauses. In the first group the information contained in the clause is essential. If the clause were removed, then the meaning of the sentence would be quite different. Imagine these sentences without their adjective clauses.

    > All public buildings *that do not have handicap access* will be reviewed.
    > Every student *who went on the field trip* became sick.
    > I'll never forget the lake in Minnesota *where I caught my first fish*.

    In the next group of examples, the adjective clause is set off from the rest of the sentence by commas. The information which the clause contains, while perhaps quite interesting, is not crucial to our understanding of the noun or pronoun it describes. Reading the sentence without the clause, we still comprehend the central message.

    > The Washington Monument, *which stands 535 feet high*, was first on our list to visit.
    > My next-door neighbor, *whose apple tree hangs over our yard*, just delivered some fresh cider.
    > We finally traded in our old Chevy, *which had nearly two hundred thousand miles on it*.

2. When the relative pronoun is replacing a direct object, that pronoun may often be omitted from the final sentence.

    > The desk *(which) we bought at the auction* had a secret compartment.
    > Everyone *(whom) we met* was very friendly.
    > I just love the hat *(that) you gave me*.

3. Knowing how an adjective clause works should help you figure out when to use *who* and *whom*. Look back over the examples and notice that *who* replaces a subject noun or pronoun, and *whom* replaces an object noun or pronoun. The words *him* and *them*, which are related to *whom*, are also in the objective case. Notice the letter *-m* at the end of all three. That's your clue.

THE ADJECTIVE CLAUSE: SAMPLES

To Jane, he could only be a man *whose proposals she had refused* and *whose merit she had undervalued.*

—Jane Austen, *Pride and Prejudice*

She was one of those persons *who have allowed their lives to be gnawed away* because they have fallen in love with an idea several centuries before its appointed appearance in the history of civilization.

—Thornton Wilder, *The Bridge of San Louis Ray*

Her mother, *who had just come downstairs,* turned to greet her father from the fireplace, *where she was kindling barked-oak twigs under the breakfast kettle.*

—Thomas Hardy, *Tess of the D'Urbervilles*

I recounted at length, in the Indian tongue, the history of our attempts to settle on Tupuai, and ended by expressing some sympathy with the people of the island, *who,* after all, *had done no more than repel what they considered an invasion of their home.*

—Charles Nordoff and James Norman Hall, *Mutiny on the Bounty*

He did not begin to calm down until he cut the tops off every camellia bush *Mrs. Dubose owned,* until the ground was littered with green buds and leaves.

—Harper Lee, *To Kill a Mockingbird*

CLAUSES

EXERCISE C: adjective clauses

Name: _____

Accuracy _____ Creativity _____

Directions: In the spaces below, write adjective clauses that modify the words in **bold** print. Try to use each relative pronoun or relative adverb at least once. Do not set off the clause with commas if it is essential. If it is not essential, you may use commas.

1. The treasure **map** _____

   _____ shows a buried treasure at the base of that sycamore tree.

2. Almost every **flavor** _____

   _____ has nuts in it.

3. I spent all day looking for **Felix** _____

   _____ .

4. My **grandmother** _____

   _____ can still beat me at tennis.

5. Are you sure this is the **restaurant** _____

   _____ ?

6. I think 2014 was the **year** _____

   _____ .

7. Most **people** _____

   _____ would have given up by now.

8. You had better have a good **reason** _____

   _____ .

9. The **salesperson** _____

   _____ said it wouldn't shrink.

10. The **circus** _____

    featured a **high-wire act** _____ .

CLAUSES

EXERCISE D: writing independent clauses

Accuracy _____ **Creativity** _____

Directions: For each sentence below, we have provided an adjective clause. You are to add an independent clause that logically and creatively might go with that adjective clause. Write out the entire sentence, and punctuate it correctly.

Example: (which broke the first time I wound it up)   I traded my lucky rabbit's foot
for this silly fire engine, *which broke the first time I wound it up.*

1. (who taught me how to tie a square knot) _____

   _____

2. (from whom she received the invitation) _____

   _____

3. (which didn't look scary at first) _____

   _____

4. (where the water was eight feet deep) _____

   _____

5. (whose name appears on the list) _____

   _____

6. (when the storm knocked down our tree house) _____

   _____

7. (that was missing two buttons) _____

   _____

8. (which got thrown out with the trash) _____

   _____

9. (whom everyone wanted to meet) _____

   _____

10. (I found) _____

    _____

CLAUSES

Name: _____

EXERCISE E: writing adjective clauses

Accuracy _____ **Creativity** _____

Directions: For each sentence below, we have provided a noun or a pronoun, followed by a relative pronoun or a relative adverb. You are to take that series of words and create a sentence that illustrates the use of the adjective clause. Pay particular attention when a comma is indicated.

Example: (notebook which)   _I finally located a notebook which will hold all my papers,_
plus my ruler, paper punch, protractor, pencils, and assignment book.

1. (music teacher whose) _____

_____

2. (hospital, where) _____

_____

3. (Charles Winters, whom) _____

_____

4. (that which) _____

_____

5. (reason why) _____

_____

6. (answer that) _____

_____

7. (holiday, when) _____

_____

8. (some who) _____

_____

9. (Route 66, which) _____

_____

10. (anyone whom) _____

_____

CLAUSES

Name: _____

EXERCISE F: reading for adjective clauses

Accuracy _____

Directions: Now, read in a good book and find three sentences containing adjective clauses. Write out the sentences below, putting parentheses around each clause. Also tell the title of the book and its author.

_____

_____

_____

_____

_____

_____

_____

_____

_____

_____

_____

_____

_____

_____

Book title: _____

Author: _____

NOUN CLAUSE

We have considered several kinds of nouns: the common noun, the proper noun, the gerund phrase, and the infinitive phrase. Now we will look at the **noun clause**, the third kind of dependent clause. A noun clause usually appears as the subject, the direct object, the object of a preposition, or the predicate noun in a sentence.

A noun clause may begin in a variety of ways: with a subordinating conjunction, with a relative pronoun, with a relative adverb, or with a relative adjective.

The **subordinating conjunctions** that begin noun clauses are *that, the fact that, if,* and *whether.*

that	+	she wasn't happy with her new job
the fact that	+	some of the silverware was missing
if	+	we could get off the train in time
whether	+	there would be enough room for both of us

Look at how these clauses function in these sentences:

subject	The fact that some of the silverware was missing made me suspicious.
direct object	I wondered *if we could get off the train in time.*
object of preposition	Her friend knew nothing except *that she wasn't happy with her new job.*
predicate noun	The question was *whether there would be enough room for both of us.*

When the noun clause is a direct object, the conjunction *that* is often omitted.

You didn't tell me *(that) you grew up on a dairy farm.*

The **relative pronouns** that begin noun clauses are *who, whom, which,* and *what,* plus their *-ever* forms:

direct object	Did you find out *who sprinkled the sneezing powder inside the tuba?*
direct object	As newcomers to the city, we didn't know *whom we could trust.*
direct object	I can't remember *which is the right direction to the museum.*
predicate noun	Our biggest problem is *what we should do with the dog this weekend.*
subject	*Whoever wins the sack race* will get this cherry pie for a prize.
subject	*Whatever you choose as your winter sport* will be fine with me.

The **relative adverbs** that begin noun clauses are *why, where, when,* and *how.*

direct object	The coach asked *why I had stayed up so late the night before the game.*
object of preposition	*From where they sat* they could see into six different states.
predicate noun	The best part was *when the tadpoles turned into frogs.*
object of preposition	There is nothing in the directions about *how you attach the wheels.*

The **relative adjectives** that begin noun clauses are *whose, which, whichever, what*, and *whatever*.

object of preposition	She grades papers by *whose handwriting is the neatest.*
direct object	The gardener asked my father *which tree he wanted removed.*
subject	*Whichever action you decide to take* must first be approved by me.
direct object	They haven't decided *what color balloons they want at the wedding.*
direct object	You go ahead and play *whatever music you want.*

NOUN CLAUSE ISSUES

1. **Noun clause or adjective clause?** Many of the words that introduce a noun clause may also be used to introduce an adjective clause: *who, whose, whom, which, that, why, where, when*, and several of the *-ever* words. The key to telling which kind of clause you are dealing with is to determine its function in the sentence. If it is performing a noun function, it is a noun clause; if it is modifying a noun or pronoun, it is an adjective clause.

noun clause, direct object	I wonder *who made those blueberry muffins.*
adjective clause, modifying *chef*	We fired the chef *who made those blueberry muffins.*

2. **Noun clause or adverb clause?** It is also easy to think that a clause beginning with *why, where, when*, or *how* would be an adverb clause, since it seems to be giving adverb-like information. But a closer look shows that the clause does not answer the question, it only raises the issue.

direct object	The clerk didn't know *why we were buying so many rubber bands.*
direct object	After three weeks we discovered *where the smell was coming from.*
object of the preposition	It was almost four hours between *when we arrived at the airport and when our flight left.*
direct object	Please tell me *how I offended you.*

To summarize, the noun clause can be tricky. Just be sure that it meets both requirements:

It's a Noun because:	it is working as a noun in the sentence
It's a Clause because:	it contains a subject and a verb

In the samples on the next page, think about what function the noun clause is performing in the sentence.

THE NOUN CLAUSE: SAMPLES

None could remember *when the little church had been so full before.*

—Mark Twain, *Tom Sawyer*

What he had in mind was a straightforward, textbook operation.

—Pierre Boulle, *The Bridge over the River Kwai*

When he was younger he was a masterful dog, and also then *what made him dangerous* was *the fact that the club of the man in the red sweater had knocked all blind puck and rashness out of his desire for mastery.*

—Jack London, *The Call of the Wild*

There was no denying *that a kiss from someone you loved was different from any other kind of kiss and should be studied up on and looked at carefully,* so you could recognize it when love came down on you.

—Ntozake Shange, *Betsy Brown*

Mrs. Gardiner and Elizabeth talked of all that had occurred during their visit, as they returned, except *what had particularly interested them both.*

—Jane Austen, *Pride and Prejudice*

Deborah had looked about and found *that she could not see except in outlines,* gray against gray, and with no depth, but flatly, like a picture.

—Hannah Green, *I Never Promised You a Rose Garden*

CLAUSES

Name: _____

EXERCISE G: writing noun clauses

Accuracy _____ **Creativity** _____

Directions: Below is a list of the words that can introduce a noun clause. Complete each sentence by selecting one of the words and then finishing the noun clause creatively. In the space after the sentence, write the appropriate letter that tells how the noun clause is being used.

that	the fact that	if	whether	
who	whose	whom	which	what
whoever	whomever	whichever	whatever	
why	where	when	how	

A=Subject   **B=Direct Object**   **C=Predicate Noun**   **D=Object of the Preposition**

Example: I just discovered <u>where my favorite band rehearses.</u> __**B**__

1. _____

   _____ makes no difference to me. _____

2. I will know by tomorrow _____

   _____ _____

3. You should ask the teacher about _____

   _____ _____

4. We all enjoyed _____ _____

   _____ _____

5. Based on _____

   _____, I've decided to forget the whole thing. _____

6. I should have guessed _____

   _____ _____

7. The only decision remaining was _____

   _____ _____

8. The doctor asked me _____

_____ _____

9. _____

_____ might be the biggest decision of your life. _____

10. I'll be satisfied with _____

_____ _____

EXERCISE H: reading for noun clauses   Accuracy _____

Directions: Now, read in a good book and find two sentences containing noun clauses. Write out the sentences below, putting parentheses around each clause. Be able to tell how each clause is being used in the sentence. Also tell the title of the book and its author.

_____

_____

_____

_____

_____

_____

_____

_____

_____

_____

_____

_____

Book title: _____

Author: _____

9. PUNCTUATION

In this book we have divided punctuation rules into **three categories**. There is **conventional punctuation**, the punctuation we use simply because it is the conventional, or customary, thing to do when we write. We put a period at the end of a sentence, commas between items in a series, and a question mark at the end of a question.

The second section is devoted to the use of **quotation marks**, which often can be complicated when conveying conversation or quoting from the works of other writers. An otherwise excellent short story or research paper can be spoiled if you do not know how to use these quotation marks correctly.

And finally there is **stylistic punctuation**, the kind that will enable you to get the most out of the grammar you have studied so far. An introductory phrase set off by a comma, a series of infinitives following a colon, a conjunctive adverb after a semicolon—punctuation and grammar go hand in hand to make your writing clear and interesting.

CONVENTIONAL PUNCTUATION

Period

At the end of a sentence	The manager has left for the day.			
After a mild command	Turn to page seventeen.			
After an abbreviation of a word or title	Mrs. ft.	Dr. etc.	Rd. Sept.	Jr. Ph.D.
Exceptions—postal codes, organizations, acronyms	CA NASA	CIA NFL	NBC UNICEF	

Exclamation Mark

After an exclamation	My, what big teeth you have!
After a strong command	Give me the ball!

Question Mark

	Where do the fish go in the winter?
After a question within a statement	My question is, Who started it?

Comma

Between items in a series (include the comma before the final conjunction)	We visited Williamsburg, Busch Gardens, and Virginia Beach.
Between adjectives before a noun	We stayed in a hot, overpriced motel.
Before a coordinating conjunction joining two independent clauses	The shows were pretty boring, but the Loch Ness Monster was fantastic!
To set off parenthetical expressions and interjections	Everyone, of course, will need a tent. Oh, I am so sorry.

Comma (continued)

To set off a noun of direct address	Mother, may I do this myself? "Yes, sir, I would like to volunteer."
To separate items in a date or address (notice no comma before the zip code)	July 4, 1976, was a big day for the United States I used to work at 362 Huron Avenue, Cambridge, MA 02138
Between a name and a title (Jr., Ph.D., M.D.), and after that title if the sentence continues	Tom Thumb, Jr., was my counselor—honest!
After the salutation of a friendly letter, and after the closing of any letter	Dear Cynthia, Dear Uncle Ray, Sincerely, Yours truly,
To avoid misreading	For my dog, food has never been a problem.
To set off a nonessential appositive	The capital of Colorado, Denver, is known as the Mile High City.

Semicolon

Between items in a series if one or more of the items contain a comma	I met Dwayne Evans, the first baseman; Charlie Fodor, the shortstop; and Lloyd Fisher, the right fielder.

Apostrophe

With the letter *s*, to form the possessive of a singular noun or indefinite pronoun, or plural noun not ending in *s*	Christie's poetry reading the hospital's address anybody's guess class's pet hamster children's entertainment
To form the possessive of a plural noun ending in *s*	boys' laughter Joneses' house Thomases' new car
To form the possessive of a singular noun of more than one syllable that ends in *s;* often may be omitted	Archimedes' Principle Odysseus' adventures
To form contractions	wasn't she'll it's
To form plurals of letters, numbers, and symbols (may be omitted if no confusion)	four 7's two *m*'s +'s the 1950s all *A*'s all *C*s

Italics (Underlining)

For books, magazines, works of art, movies, ships, and the like	*The Old Man and the Sea Time* *The Secret Garden Mona Lisa* *Pinta*
For words, numbers, and letters, when referred to as such	There were five *good's* in that paragraph. There are three *4s* in my telephone number. You reversed the *i* and the *e*.

Colon

In expressions of time, and after the salutation of a business letter	We will meet at 7:30 P.M. Dear Senator Bradley:
To indicate "note what follows"	Here's what I want you to do: stay down and keep me covered.

Hyphen

To split a word at the end of a typed line	The pole fell down and the telephone company replaced it.
With the prefixes *self-* and *all-*, with the suffix *-elect*, with all prefixes before a proper noun or a proper adjective	self-appointed all-league chairman-elect pre-Columbian pro-Canadian non-Asian
For compound numbers from twenty-one to ninety-nine; with fractions and compound adjectives when written before the noun they modify (except with an *-ly* adverb	fifty-three one hundred fifty-two a three-quarters majority fifty-year-old car fur-lined jacket neatly stacked firewood

Quotation marks

For slang expressions	said it was "for the birds"
For ironic purposes	called his old car his "limo"
For titles of short stories, poems, songs, chapter titles, magazine or newspaper articles, and other short writings	"The Gift of the Magi" "The Owl and the Pussycat" "White Christmas" "Selecting the Best Dog for You" "My Summer Vacation"

Notice that these shorter (**quick**) written pieces would usually appear within larger works—a novel, a literary collection, a magazine or newspaper. **Long** works would be underlined or written in italics. (see **Italics**, above)

Quick = Quotes   Long = Line

However, use underlining for titles only when writing by hand. When writing on a computer, use italics, not underlining.

PUNCTUATION

Name: _____

EXERCISE A: reading for conventional punctuation

Accuracy: _____

Directions: Read in a good magazine and try to locate sentences that demonstrate conventional punctuation. Try to find one example of each of the following uses of punctuation, then write each sentence in the space labeled with the corresponding letter. If the sentence you have found is long, write out just enough to make your illustration clear.

(A) apostrophe for possessive of singular noun
(B) apostrophe for a contraction
(C) period for an abbreviation
(D) comma between items in a series
(E) comma to set off a parenthetical expression

(F) commas to set off an appositive
(G) italics for any reason
(H) colon to indicate "note what follows"
(I) hyphen for a compound adjective
(J) quotation marks for a title

(A) _____

_____

(B) _____

_____

(C) _____

_____

(D) _____

_____

(E) _____

_____

(F) _____

_____

(G) _____

_____

(H) _____

_____

(I) _____

_____

(J) _____

_____

Magazine Title and Date: _____

PUNCTUATION

Name: _____

EXERCISE B: conventional punctuation   **Accuracy** _____ **Creativity** _____

Directions: Fill in the blanks as directed, then punctuate the completed sentences as necessary.

1. Three candidates were on the ballot James Koslowski _____
    (nonessential appositive)

    Deborah Frasure _____ and Maureen Sarmanian
                    (nonessential appositive)

2. _____ do you remember who sang _____
    (noun of direct address)   *(song title)*

    _____ back in the _____ Grace asked
                                                   (decade)

3. _____ grandmother was born in _____ _____
    (possessive noun)   *(city)*   *(country)*

    on _____ _____ _____
       (month)   *(day)*   *(year)*

4. _____ Jeremiah Boylan _____ will give a lecture entitled _____
    (abbreviated title)   *(abbreviated title)*   *(short written piece)*

    _____ at the annual meeting of the _____
                                                                   (acronym)

5. Gail announced in the school newspaper _____ the editor
                                           (appositive–name of the newspaper)

    _____ referred to the food served in the cafeteria as _____
    (nonessential appositive)   *(slang or ironic expression)*

6. My favorite artist _____ painted _____
                       (nonessential appositive)   *(hyphenated number)*

    versions of his famous work _____
                                (essential appositive)

7. You know the history teacher said you really _____ use the word _____
                                                 (contraction)   *(word used as a word)*

    so often or you will put your reader to sleep

8. _____ these _____ _____
         (interjection)   *(adjective)*   *(compound adjective)*

    souvenirs are fantastic my mother exclaimed

9. Is the first chapter of _____ favorite novel
                           (possessive of noun ending with the letter s*)*

   _____ called _____
           (title of novel)   *(title of chapter)*

10. I got two _____ on my report card Alison bragged
           (letter grades)

QUOTATION MARKS

Often the most difficult punctuation to work with is quotation marks. Besides being used to identify such items as slang words or short stories, they also enclose direct quotations of what people say or write. In conversation, people talk about stories, ask questions, shout, whisper; in writing, authors mention books, cite dates, quote other authors. With all these marks of punctuation going on at once, it can get quite complicated.

Here are three additional situations in which quotation marks are used and require your attention.

1. **Writing conversation:** When you write a story, you will often want to include a conversation. The words of your characters will be mixed in with your own narrative, using such phrases as *she said* or *I replied* or *he yelled*. These phrases might introduce the quotation, or fall somewhere in the middle, or end it. Follow these rules:

    a. Use commas to separate what you write from the quoted material
    b. Capitalize the first word of the quotation
    c. Always put the comma or period inside the closing quotation mark

Examples:

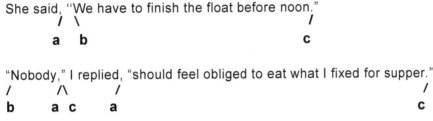

She said, "We have to finish the float before noon."

"Nobody," I replied, "should feel obliged to eat what I fixed for supper."

"Let's hope he remembered to bring the rings," the bride whispered.

2. **Quoting from sources:** When you write an essay, you may wish to quote an author's exact words, and the quotations will be mixed in with your text. Follow the same rules that you use for writing conversation.

Examples:

Lincoln said, "A house divided against itself cannot stand."

"Uranium," the encyclopedia explains, "was named after the planet Uranus."

"The only thing we have to fear is fear itself," Franklin Roosevelt warned.

An important variation to these rules occurs when you take only a fragment of the original quotation and incorporate it into your own sentence.

Charles Dickens established the theme of contrasts when he wrote that 1775 was "the best of times" as well as "the worst of times."

The first sentence of Charles Dickens' novel *A Tale of Two Cities* is "It was the best of times, it was the worst of times." Rule **b** does not apply in our example, because we have quoted only parts from within the original sentence. Rule **a** does not apply, because the quotations are actually part of the sentence, as predicate nouns, and not separate from it. Rule **c** still applies.

3. **Quotation marks with other punctuation:** Let's add the other forms of punctuation one by one and see what happens. Fortunately, italics (underlining), apostrophes, and hyphens do not have any effect on our use of quotation marks.

Semicolon, colon, or dash   always goes outside the closing quotation mark

He called me "shrimp face"; that's when I knew I was in trouble.

We should bring one thing as an "intimidator": a water pistol filled to the brim.

"Cool," "groovy, "with it"—all were popular when I was your age.

Question mark or exclamation mark   goes inside if the quote is a question or exclamation
goes outside if the quote is not, but the larger sentence is

"Do you remember what she was wearing?" the inspector asked.

Did anyone ever ask you, "What historical person would you most like to meet?"

Did anyone ever say to you, "You remind me of Octavia Spencer"?

"Watch out for the bull!" the farmer yelled.

I'll never again come to one of your little "gatherings"!

4. **Quotation marks within quotation marks:** On rare occasions, you will need to write one set of quoted material inside another. Perhaps one person is quoting a friend; perhaps a lecturer is talking about a poem; perhaps an author is referring to a scientific essay.

  Whatever the reason, use a **single quotation mark** (apostrophe) for the innermost quoted material. All other punctuation rules remain in effect.

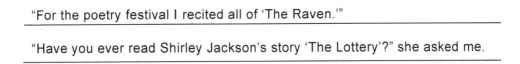

"For the poetry festival I recited all of 'The Raven.'"

"Have you ever read Shirley Jackson's story 'The Lottery'?" she asked me.

QUOTATION MARKS ISSUES

1. **Quotations in dialogue:** If you are writing a conversation between two or more characters, give each speaker his or her own paragraph in turn.

2. **Quotations of more than one paragraph in dialogue:** If a spoken quotation continues for more than one paragraph, here's what to do:

    a. Begin the quotation with an opening quotation mark.

    b. Do not put a closing quotation mark at the end of the paragraph.

    c. Put an opening quotation mark at the beginning of the next paragraph, to show that the quoted material continues.

    d. Continue this pattern until the quotation finishes. Then close the quote.

3. **Unspoken words:** If a character *wonders* or *thinks* a thought, treat it as though it were actually spoken.

  "I sure hope I forgot to lock the back door," I thought as I headed around the house.

4. **Long citations in an essay:** If you are quoting from a resource such as an encyclopedia, essay, or other academic reference, you might want to quote several lines. If the citation will occupy more than four lines, indent the quotation from the left and right margins and do not use quotation marks. Indenting signals to the reader that this is a quotation.

  Single space if you have been double spacing.

PUNCTUATION

Name: _____

EXERCISE C: punctuation in conversation

Accuracy _____ **Creativity** _____

This is a chance to show off what you know about punctuation. Using the space below and on the back, write a scene from a story in which two friends are talking. You may provide whatever narration you wish, such as how they are speaking or what happens next. They might be discussing books or news or people. Along with quotation marks to indicate their conversation, try to use several illustrations of conventional punctuation. The conversation should make sense, but it does not have to be a finished piece. **Tip:** You may like to use page 102 to jot down some ideas.

_____

_____

_____

_____

_____

_____

_____

_____

_____

_____

_____

_____

_____

_____

_____

_____

STYLISTIC PUNCTUATION

Stylistic punctuation is the result, not so much of *what* you are writing, but of *how* you are writing. It is the punctuation you use to assemble your sentence structures, combining the phrases and clauses that give variety and life to all you write. It is important to gain confidence with these forms of punctuation so that you may take full advantage of all the grammar you have learned.

Comma

After any introductory participial phrase, infinitive phrase, more than one prepositional phrase, or adverb clause:

Stepping off the bus, I twisted my ankle.

Played by a professional violinist, his new composition didn't sound so bad.

To avoid the crush of the crowd, we just sat in our seats after the movie finished.

Like a kitten with a catnip mouse, the baby played with her new rattle.

Although we had practiced that play fifty times, we couldn't do it in the big game.

To set off nonessential phrases or clauses:

Nonessential phrases and clauses are modifiers which, although usually quite interesting and informative, may still be omitted without preventing a reader's understanding of the sentence. The reader will still know what you mean, because the information is common knowledge or because the situation is clear for some other reason.

If the modifier is essential, do not set it off with commas. It usually is essential when it isolates one or a few from a larger group.

Alice Walker's third novel, *The Color Purple*, won the Pulitzer Prize.
(an author can have only one third novel; the title is informative but not essential)

Edgar Allan Poe's short story "The Tell-Tale Heart" contains magnificent punctuation.
(Poe wrote many short stories; this title is essential to tell which one you mean)

Fred Tartakoff, who works in the quarry, writes poetry as a hobby.
(the proper noun identifies him; the adjective clause is not essential)

Everyone who works in the quarry has to pass a rigid safety exam.
(not everyone takes the test; the adjective clause is essential to narrow the meaning)

I couldn't find the tent which served as the first-aid station.
(there were many tents; the adjective clause separates the one from many)

To separate phrases or clauses in a series:

You know that a conventional use of the comma is to separate items such as nouns or adjectives in a series. Likewise, you should separate a series of phrases or clauses, remembering to put a comma before the final conjunction.

We wandered around the woods aimlessly, stumbling over tree roots, scraping ourselves on rocks, and getting more frightened by the minute.

The lawyer tried to prove that the defendant was not in the city on the night in question, that he did not know the injured party, and that he did not own a car.

Semicolon

Between two closely related independent clauses not joined by a coordinating conjunction:

You should have been here this morning; you would have understood why I got upset.

Between two independent clauses joined by a coordinating conjunction, if there are other commas in the sentence that might cause confusion:

I've been to Tampa, Miami, Daytona Beach, and Orlando; but Sanibel is still the best.

Before a conjunctive adverb joining two independent clauses (see page 38):

She forgot to put a stamp on the letter; nevertheless, the post office still delivered it.

Colon

Before a formal statement or quotation; to introduce a list or an explanation or elaboration of what has already been said:

I'll never forget that one recurring line in his speech: "Stealing is stealing."

For the recipe you will need the following: four eggs, three cups of flour, a cup of milk, half a stick of butter, and a tablespoon of vanilla.

Dash

Before an explanation to imply "in other words," to indicate an abrupt break in thought, or after an introductory series:

We could see the whole town below us—the track at the high school, the town swimming pool, even the golden arches.

I had to save her—she was my best friend—so I just jumped right in.

Bribes, pleadings, threats—nothing could make him change his mind.

Parentheses

To set off supplementary ideas, explanations, or "whispered" asides:

A conjunctive adverb joins two independent clauses (see page 38).

Three boxes of cookies (there are two dozen in each box) should be enough.

The lead actor (remind me to look up his name) talked just like Bugs Bunny.

PUNCTUATION

Name: _____

EXERCISE D: stylistic punctuation

Accuracy _____ **Creativity** _____

Directions: Fill in the blank spaces with sentences of your own creation, according to the punctuation and directions given.

1. _____ ;
(independent clause)

_____ , _____ .
(conjunctive adverb)   *(independent clause)*

2. _____ ,
(independent clause)

_____ .
(nonessential adjective clause)

3. _____ :
(independent clause)

_____ ,
(infinitive phrase)

_____ , and finally
(infinitive phrase)

_____ .
(infinitive phrase)

4. _____ — _____
(begin the independent clause)   *(abrupt break)*

_____ — _____ .
     (finish the independent clause)

5. _____
(independent clause)

_____ (_____) .
     (whispered aside or explanation)

6. _____ , _____ ,
(first item)   *(second item)*

_____ — all _____ .
(third item)   *(finish the sentence)*

7. _____ , _____
   (proper noun)   *(nonessential adjective clause)*

   _____ , _____ .
                                    (finish the sentence)

8. _____ , _____
   (two consecutive prepositional phrases)

   _____ .
                    (independent clause)

9. _____ ;
                    (independent clause)

   _____ .
                    (independent clause)

10. _____
                    (independent clause)

   _____ , _____
                                    (nonessential appositive)

   _____ .

10. WRITING PATTERNS

Consider the following sentence:

> The trapeze artist swung high above the crowd.

We are told here that a certain event is taking place, but we don't really experience it for ourselves. We feel little of the excitement; we don't see colors or smell the peanuts; we know nothing of *why* or *how*.

Remember "Show and Tell" in elementary school? You were always more interested in what was being shown than told. So it should be in your writing. And you can use many of the grammatical constructions you have learned to create vivid, specific images for your reader.

One of the interesting features of many phrases and clauses is that they may be placed at more than one location in the sentence. Look again at the example above and consider the many places where modifiers may be added: We have inserted numbers to show the possible locations for each of the modifiers. For example, the adjectives *handsome and daring* could be written either at location (1) or (2).

> (1) The trapeze artist (2) swung (3) high above the crowd (4).

Adjectives:	handsome and daring (1, 2)
Adverbs:	gracefully, rhythmically, almost magically (1, 3, 4)
Prepositional phrase:	in a costume of gold and green (1, 2, 4)
Appositive:	the circus's star performer (1, 2, 4)
Present participial phrase:	curling his legs around the ropes (1, 2, 4)
Past participial phrase:	inspired by the applause below (1, 2, 4)
Infinitive phrase:	to draw the audience's attention (1, 2, 4)
Adjective clause:	for whom the audience had been waiting (2)
Adverb clause:	even though he had finished his routine (1, 4)

You should notice several things at this point. First, you see that the adjective clause can go in one position only, immediately after the noun it modifies. Second, in most cases, but not always, the modifier will be set off from the main clause by a comma. Your knowledge of commas, especially those involving essential and nonessential modifiers, should enable you to determine whether a comma is appropriate. And third, beware the possibility of a misplaced modifier. If the original sentence had read *The trapeze artist swung toward his partner*, several of the above modifiers would take on different meanings as you moved them around the sentence.

We can enrich our sentences further by using, not one modifier, but several, in the sentence. First, we may use different modifiers in different places.

> Handsome and daring, the trapeze artist, in a costume of gold and green, swung high above the crowd.

We may also use more than one of the same type of modifier consecutively.

> The trapeze artist swung high above the crowd, curling his legs around
> the ropes and waving to the ringmaster below.

Or we may use different modifiers consecutively, with the second modifier telling about something in the first modifier, or summarizing the overall sentence.

> The trapeze artist swung high above the crowd, gracefully, rhythmically, almost magically,
> like the pendulum of a human clock.

> The trapeze artist swung high above the crowd, inspired by the applause below, even
> though it was his third performance of the day.

WRITING PATTERNS

Name: _____

EXERCISE A

Accuracy _____ Creativity _____

Directions: Fill in the blank spaces below with modifiers, as indicated, that would make the sentence below more vivid and interesting. Also write the numbers telling where those modifiers might be placed in the sentence.

(1) The children (2) ran (3) to the merry-go-round (4).

Adjectives: _____

_____

Adverbs: _____

_____

Prepositional phrase: _____

_____

Appositive: _____

_____

Present participial phrase: _____

_____

Past participial phrase: _____

_____

Infinitive phrase _____

_____

Adjective clause: _____

_____

Adverb clause: _____

_____

WRITING PATTERNS

Name: _____

EXERCISE B

Accuracy _____ Creativity _____

Directions: Fill in the blank spaces below with modifiers, as indicated, that would make the sentence below more vivid and interesting. Also write the numbers telling where those modifiers might be placed in the sentence.

(1) The old carpenter (2) paused in his work (3).

Adjectives: _____

_____

Adverbs: _____

_____

Prepositional phrase: _____

_____

Appositive: _____

_____

Present participial phrase: _____

_____

Past participial phrase: _____

_____

Infinitive phrase _____

_____

Adjective clause: _____

_____

Adverb clause: _____

_____

WRITING PATTERNS

Name: _____

EXERCISE C

Accuracy _____ **Creativity** _____

Directions: Fill in the blank spaces below with modifiers, as indicated, that would make the sentence below more vivid and interesting. Also write the numbers telling where those modifiers might be placed in the sentence.

(1) Sharon (2) dropped her favorite sweater (3) on the chair (4).

Adjectives: _____

_____

Adverbs: _____

_____

Prepositional phrase: _____

_____

Appositive: _____

_____

Present participial phrase: _____

_____

Past participial phrase: _____

_____

Infinitive phrase _____

_____

Adjective clause: _____

_____

Adverb clause: _____

_____

WRITING PATTERNS

Name: _____

EXERCISE D

Accuracy _____ **Creativity** _____

Directions: Fill in the blank spaces below with modifiers, as indicated, that would make the sentence below more vivid and interesting. Also write the numbers telling where those modifiers might be placed in the sentence.

(1) The burglar (2) lifted the window (3).

Adjectives: _____

_____

Adverbs: _____

_____

Prepositional phrase: _____

_____

Appositive: _____

_____

Present participial phrase: _____

_____

Past participial phrase: _____

_____

Infinitive phrase _____

_____

Adjective clause: _____

_____

Adverb clause: _____

_____

WRITING PATTERNS

Name: _____

EXERCISE E

Accuracy _____ **Creativity** _____

Directions: Now that you have practiced using different modifiers with single sentences, try writing a scene from a story that continues to use these writing patterns. Select any one of the situations you have written about in the previous four exercises—the children, the carpenter, Sharon, or the burglar—as a starting point, and expand it into an interesting piece that demonstrates your confidence with the grammar and the writing techniques you have studied. There's no need for a full story, just a really well-done scene.

_____

_____

_____

_____

_____

_____

_____

_____

_____

_____

_____

_____

_____

_____

_____

_____

_____

_____

_____

_____

CPSIA information can be obtained
at www.ICGtesting.com
Printed in the USA
LVHW011459010922
727308LV00008B/535